The Night of Swaying Grass:
A Memoir in Poems

by R. Diskin Black

Copyright 2025 R. Diskin Black
ISBN: 978-1-957863-55-9

Please comply with copyright laws and do not reproduce, scan, photograph, or distribute this book in any form without permission from the author and/or publisher. (Though we do encourage quoting your favorite lines with proper citation in book reviews or referencing this book, again with proper citation, in academic research.) Parisian Phoenix does not support the use of our intellectual property for the training of artificial training intelligence technologies or systems.

The author, publisher and artists involved with the production of this book appreciate reader support.

Cover Design: Tariq Danzig, tariqdanzig.com

Parisian Phoenix Publishing, Easton, Pennsylvania

"R. Diskin Black's poems are surprising the way a sudden rainstorm in bright sunshine is surprising. They make the reader stop and sense, vividly, the meaning of "cat" and "lips" and "sorrow" and "sharing." These poems are tender, moving, sometimes written from a child's perspective, sometimes from a sad young man's, finally from an older man's, who still looks out through all the other perspectives, with warmth, loss, fear, and a kind of innocent joy. What joins the poems is a deep, unspoken conviction that I can only articulate as something like "all human beings are innocent" or "love is the only important meaning there is." This book is beautiful, and whole."

— **Donna Minkowitz**, author of *Donnaville, Growing Up Golem,* and *Ferocious Romance.*

"There's a little Antoine de Saint-Exupery in this collection, a feeling of a child passing through time and space. New York and the carnage of AIDS, the wonderment and anguish of life, the beatitudes and horrors of George Floyd's murder, bodies in the streets, sex, sweat, loving, protesting. Our lives are an epiphany. We are plopped here with no explanation why, losing parents, friends, animals in the process. So, what's to be done? Read a poem in a garden. Demand joy despite despair. This memoir told in poems by R. Diskin Black reminds us of the mystery of it all."

— **Benjamin Heim Shepard**, author of *White Nights and Ascending Shadows, From ACT UP to the WTO, The Beach Beneath the Streets, Play, Creativity and Social Movements, Queer Political Performance and Protest, Rebel Friendships,Illuminations on Market Street: (a Story about Sex and Estrangement, AIDS and Loss, and Other Preoccupations in San Francisco), Community Projects as Social Activism, Brooklyn Tides: On the Fall and Rise of a Global Borough, Sustainable Urbanism, Travels in a Conflicted World,* and *On Friendship, Activism, and Fighting.*

"63 poems and 63 years embody *The Night of Swaying Grass*, a singular journey – in turns poignant and hilarious, often both – from the author who was born in '63. From a prodigiously self-aware New Jersey childhood longing for a lost *Tír na nÓg* to finding political/sexual/spiritual liberation in the late 1980s West Village — the epicenter of ACT UP activism — these poems powerfully evoke that explosive era's street scenes as well as tenderly invoke the plaintive, inner hardships endured and triumphs earned along his beautifully recounted road. Every phrase, reverie and tableau is pointed and purposeful, vivid and visceral. I first met R. Diskin Black in the 2000s as a student in one of my playwriting workshops. We reconnected in the 2010s through our activism with Rise and Resist (which grew out of ACT UP). In the 2020s, it is an honor to blurb his book as fellow authors. I know you will be as moved by this unique collection of a life in verse and a verse o' life as much I was and continue to be."

– **Alvin Eng**, writer, educator, acoustic punk raconteur and author of the memoir, *Our Laundry, Our Town*.

"Reading *The Night in Swaying Grass* is like sharing a wonderful dinner with a wise and cherished friend. R. Diskin Black has given us an intimate, often surprising, and always beautifully told story of innocence, grief, self-discovery, and resilience. Whether recalling the young boy clinging to the earth while struggling to understand the early death of his father, the young man refusing to look away from a beautiful, lesioned stranger and finding his community in activism, or the middle-aged survivor searching for ways to live with his "memory-beetles" while yearning for spiritual and physical connection during the dark days of the COVID pandemic, Black leads us through the traumas of the last sixty years with a tender and forgiving touch. I want to order another bottle of wine and read some more."

— **Ron Goldberg**, author of *Boy with the Bullhorn: A Memoir and History of ACT UP New York*

For

Richard,

Stephen,

Howard,

my parents,

and all the departed,

including Clancy, Ginger,

Barnaby, Jasper, Godzilla, & Ozzzy

And There Was Evening (An Erasure Poem)

In the beginning
        God created
            the
                formless void and darkness

                          while a wind
  swept over

      the light;
             the darkness
                  was
                       the first day.
And God said,
      Let there be
          in the midst of
             evening
  the dry
      Earth
          yielding
             yielding.
And there was evening.
And God said,
      Let
        the night
           be for seasons and for days
                  and years,
        and let
          the night
             rule over the day and over the night
                 and the darkness.
And there was evening.

And God
        created the great
                monsters
                        and
                              God
                                    blessed them,
                                              saying,
Be fruitful and multiply on the earth.
And there was evening.
                          And God said,
Let   every   creeping
                    thing
                          creep upon
                                humankind
    and
        wild
                  creep
upon the earth
                and
                    have dominion over
                                  every living thing that moves.
God said
             yield
                      to every beast of the earth
                              and everything that
                    creeps.
And it was so.
God saw everything that he had made, and indeed,
                                      there
                                      was
                                          evening.

Source material: *The Book of Genesis* [1:1-1:31]

Chapter 1. I AM BORN

Will I turn out to be the hero of my life?
It's too soon to say.
I record that I was born on a Thursday
Three weeks late leaving the womb
Arriving in JFK's Camelot during its last days,
Among the youngest of the boomers
To ever enter most rooms.
While my mother
Induced by scopolamine and morphine
Slumbered in a 1963 twilight birth sleep,
I bid farewell to my friend the placenta
Twisting and turning head-first moving through the birth canal,
As my lateness indicated
Not eager for this incarnation to begin in the least.
Perhaps not so clueless I was about to dance
A late 20th into 21st century ballet
Brimming with plague and lost people and environmental dismay,
I let out a scream
They're still hearing in New Jersey to this day.
Unlike young Copperfield
No nurse or neighborhood sage
Declared me destined for an unlucky life
Between this birth and the grave.
But like David C
I would know spirits and ghosts
In good times and strife
Who would show up each morning
With the buttery cinnamon toast
And linger each evening past bedtime
Swinging blithely from my intricately-carved wooden bedposts.
Though I may be confusing all the Dickens
They made me read in high school.
Ghosts past, present, future often invaded my Bildungsroman,
Which when I think back on it wasn't that cool.

In the end, mine's a story with a lot of characters coming and
    going,
A journey
Some hardship
Enough happiness
Ultimately acceptance
And self-knowing.

On a Grassy Hill

Two little boys stand on a grassy hill
Next to a hospital
Holding hands.
Their mother, close to them, points up
Toward a window
On the fifth floor.
Children aren't allowed on cancer wards in 1969.
The April wind picks up
Shaking violently nearby trees
In full bud-bursting bloom
Announcing springtime rebirth has arrived.
The bigger boy grips the smaller boy
Steadying him against the wind
Both their free hands waving
Waving
Waving
Waving
Waving
Up toward the window
Where a figure
Identified as their dad
Returns the waving
Waving
Waving
Waving
Waving
Like the violently shaking trees.
The little boys' arms become sore and tired
From this determined ceaseless flailing in the air.
Neither boy understands
Why life has brought them to this grassy hill
Marking them
As children who cannot see their father
But can wave up at him
Assured by their mother he is waving back.

This is good practice
Actually
For all the years ahead.

My Father's Arms

My father's arms were big,
Upper arms
Forearms
Wrists
Hands,
Thirty-two bones (each) like most humans,
Nerves
Blood vessels — arteries and veins —
Muscles
Skin and hair.
My earliest memory are those arms,
A place I have longed to return.
When I was five years old, I would climb up into my father's lap
To feel his arms wrapped around me
Sighing with contentment as I nested in their enveloping flesh.
On my father's left arm he had a tattoo
Acquired while a paratrooper
One thrilling reckless night during World War II.
I would trace that tattoo with my small fingers,
A picture book for me on my father's arm,
Then work my fingers under the twisting metal band of his
    wristwatch,
Resting them there
As if I was safe from the passage of time
So long as I held on to my father's watch.

One year later
The summer of '69
Months after the cancer diagnosis came
My father's robust arms
Began to wither and die
Like the man attached to them.
I lingered by his bedside as he faded away
Hesitant to trace his tattoo anymore
With my shaking little-boy finger,

Hesitant to feel his strong arms
Now weak,
Embracing death
Instead of embracing me.
The absence of a wristwatch,
Always on his forearm
Below the war tattoo
There for me to touch
And stand still time,
Made his arm seem vulnerable
To the approaching end of days.
The tattoo cannot mount a defense on its own, I thought.
It needs the watch to put up a fight
Since the enemy is time
Tick
Tick
Ticking away
The last hours, minutes, seconds
My father gets to live on Earth.

Everything Will Be Okay

I take me by the hand
As one takes a child
Helping them cross the street
Guiding them
Protecting them
Holding on to them.
I am 60
I am 6 years old,
My little boy,
I'm only a boy
Watching my father
Die at home
Slowly
During the summer of '69.
I am always nearby me
In a crowd
On a bench
Sitting in the room still dark when I first enter.
I am anchored in that summer
Tending to the little boy
Who only wants to hold a grown man's hand
And feel for a moment what it's like to say Dad
To someone who's standing right there.

The days wind back round one another
And I lurk invisible in the corner of the room
People coming and going
My mother young turning old
As I watch the end of everything planned by them
For the rest of our lives.
Here I am
Slinking from the hallway
Lingering in the door jamb
Afraid of my dying father
Afraid of the dying.

It's okay, little guy,
You are a wondrous and much-loved boy.
I am a wondrous and much-loved boy.
Run out to the woods
Just beyond the house
And invent a world
Inside my head
That makes us both feel safe.
I know that's what I'll do because I remember what I did.

He walks up and touches our father's arm before leaving the bedside,
His father
My father
Our father
Who aren't yet in Heaven
Hallowed be thy name.
Good boy,
I say to him
I say to me,
Everything will be okay.

The Night of Swaying Grass

Children can see things.
The night my father died
I refused to enter the house
Plopping my six-year-old self
Among the fireflies and nighttime insects
In the tall uncut late-summer grass.
Sitting cross-legged amidst the swaying green blades
I tried to hide my tiny body
From the ghosts that descended
And attached themselves all round our roof.
In this pocket universe where I now had to live
The lawn was overgrown with fluxweed and dandelions
Since no one had revved up the power mower for months
While the business of dying was at hand.
My mother,
Standing at the open door,
Worn out
Grief-stricken
Eyes red from hours of crying,
Coaxed
Cajoled
Begged me to come inside.
But I could see the spectral beings dancing on the shingles above
And knew one of them was my father's ghost
Whom I could not trust to behave as he did
When he lived still in his kind human skin.
I clawed at the ground with both my small hands
Determined to remain anchored to earth.
I would have nothing to do with those dancing rooftop spirits
Who arrived in such numbers
Like nothing I'd ever seen before,
A multitude of shadows from some country called Heaven
I'd been told about earlier that week
When it became clear to my broken-hearted mother
The cancer had finally won.

My daddy was gone
He was now one of them
Another phantom of the gables
Cavorting in the sky
Dancing away from our house
Toward the verdant trees
Of the forest past our yard.
I watched them depart
As I'd watched them arrive,
From deep within the safe tall swaying grass,
A thousand ghosts escorting my father
To an Elysian place I didn't want to go
Beyond the explosive shaking angry trees,
Which bent first in one direction
Then the other
From the sheer force of these thousand wild unpredictable ghosts.
I remained hidden deep within the lawn turned meadow
Holding two fistfuls of dirt
Watching the Great Departure
As it left me a fatherless son,
Protected only by fireflies hovering in the warm evening air
And the mournful swaying of uncut summertime grass.

Gate of Heaven

As a child I lived with shame because my father died
Like it was a shortcoming on my part, clearly my fault,
A punishment for some uncertain crime
That would chip away over the years at my sense of self-worth.
I must have done something for him to vanish,
Leaving behind his worn-out corpse
For us to bury at Gate of Heaven Cemetery
The day my father rode through town in a hearse.
Row upon row of tombstones
Many of them chiseled with a cross
Mixed among the shady elms and happy squirrels scurrying about,
An endless sea of white granite slabs and gaudy mausoleums,
A Levittown for the expired,
Ample postwar housing for the lost.
Where was Blue Oyster Cult singing "(Don't Fear) The Reaper"
    when I needed it most
As I wandered past my grandparents and my dad
Taking note of dates of birth, dates of death
Doing math in my head
Calculating who had suffered more than me
The boy with the parent who was dead?
There was a little girl buried in the shade
Who'd been in the ground since '63.
She left this world as I arrived
My tiny brain observed.
Was it possible she returned as me?
There was also a soldier buried in our row
Twenty years before the girl
When they first declared this track of land
Would be where dead people dwelled.
My father was a soldier, too,
Also in 1943,
Jumping out of airplanes onto islands in the Pacific
Like Borneo, Guam and New Guinea.
As he gripped his parachute

Falling skillfully from the sky
Did my father ever drift past the young lieutenant buried nearby?
The little girl
The young lieutenant
Along with many passed-on others
Became a neighborhood in a way
Albeit a far cry from Mr. Rogers',
More like the third act in a community theater production
    of *Our Town*,
Where I tried to make sense of what happened to me
To my brother
And our mother,
Our beautiful mother,
Gentle, kind, knocked down.
Hail Mary
Full of grace
We prayed,
Please hold up and help our mother.

Falling from the Sky

They told me my father fought in a war
Jumping out of planes over Pacific islands from '42 to '44.
Part of a reconnaissance brigade
He parachuted into jungles and swamps
Before other allied soldiers arrived,
Scoping out enemy ambush
Finding ways for islands to be taken and infrastructure rise.
After he departed, I searched for solace and meaning,
Including in the sky,
But since I was 6 when he died
I didn't know it was solace and meaning I desired.
On those late summer days that turned into fall
I squinted at the sun
Studying each airplane that flew above
Waiting for a hatch to open
A dot to appear against the blue
That got bigger as it plunged toward ground,
Speeding downward with ferocious velocity
Until a cord was pulled and whoosh
A parachute deployed
Blooming like a dahlia
Slowing the descending dot
As it became a man
Gliding effortlessly
Dancing a sky ballet
Falling with purpose
Aiming for our house and woodsy lot.
I was falling, too,
Up toward him
Gravity suspended
So I could meet my dad,
Then clasp hands
And fall together to our yard.
I was falling anyway,
A little boy standing in the grass

While dropping from the sky
Without a cord
Without a chute
Without dancing a graceful ballet as I plummeted toward earth.
I looked and waited
Searching amidst the clouds above.
While planes appeared every day
Cruising halfway between the birds and God
No man ever jumped from one and hurtled down to me.

First Eclipse

The alignment of three celestial bodies
A thing called syzygy
Does not happen every day.
When it does it feels to me a little like sorcery.
I know it's science that explains an eclipse
But since my first one was engineered by the dead
I tend to work from a slightly skewed script,
Not exactly fearing apocalypse,
Believing more that when darkness arrives during daylight
It is the departed who've orchestrated bringing on the night.
March 7th, 1970,
Up and down the eastern U.S.
From Florida to New Jersey to Massachusetts
On my mother's birthday when she turned 45
Six months after my father died
A 95% totality solar eclipse arrived.

It was a bright winter Saturday, I recall.
Grief in our snug bungalow ranch still dripped down the walls
Stranding my mother, my brother, myself in eternal duskfall.
My mother's sister, our beloved Aunt Flo,
Pulled up to the house in her '63 Chevrolet wagon
As always, ready to go,
For months single-handedly dragging us from a strong undertow.
Flo forced us to put on coats and hats and shoes
Determined we would see the solar shroud
About to blanket the town dark Prussian blue.
I grabbed my eclipse viewbox made at school
And together the four of us ventured out
To glimpse once again the end of the world
From high atop Eagle Rock.

Flo drove the station wagon up to the Reservation
On the First Watchung Mountain
Overlooking the skyline of gritty Manhattan
With newborn Twin Towers rising and anchoring the island.

Standing near a cloud of stoned hippies gathered for the sight,
Recalling my father bringing me there for a hike,
This place of before-time memories
I no longer much liked.
I stood drenched in sorrow
My eyes pressed to a box
As the sky transformed
Casting nighttime shadows across Eagle Rock,
The air increasingly chilled with the absence of light.
I sensed excitement reverberating person to person
Through the modest-sized crowd,
Then began to reconsider what was happening out loud.
This was my father
Saying happy birthday to my mother,
I announced with my head still facing the box.

Inside I was thinking something far more complex.
My dad was telling us
Me and my brother
His death was no small thing.
It was enormous
And called for the obliteration of afternoon
With the sun's banishing.
I watched the eclipse via my art class contraption,
Mittenless hands stinging raw in icy air.
Not hearing a reply to my eclipse proclamation,
I decided to believe
Anyway
My dad remained there,
Hovering
Fluttering
Soaring,
His gargantuan wingspan
Blocking the sun,
Ushering darkness
And cold
Everywhere.

My Locust Summer

I fled into the woods after my father died
Seeking the solace of trees and rocks and celestial sunbeams
Penetrating the canopy of leaves a mile above me in the sky.
The woods behind our house cradled me then,
Becoming sometimes other planets
Though mainly this planet reimagined as a place where
    no one died,
Or rather everyone died every day
But dying meant just walking to the adjoining room
Where the next adventure waited,
Laid out on the bed like a woodland faerie costume I could wear.

In 1970, as I crept from 6 to 7,
I became many things I never was supposed to be
While the woods transformed by me
Morphed into starships and battlefields,
Castles and jungles,
Ancient forests and future moonscapes.
Among the old-growth oaks and elms I imagined violence
Savage and brutal
As both a boy and a girl,
My lifetimes bleeding together following the shock
    of childhood loss.

I was a temporary sentry of those woods behind the house,
Lucky and unlucky at once (as all people always are),
Because I was there when the soil opened for a Great Emergence
And prehistoric creatures crawled from the dirt
Seventeen-year cicadas buried since 1953
To serenade each other an insect opera,
A melody which reverberated throughout our neighborhood
Drowning out even the birds and the bees,
Inspiring Bob Dylan to write that year
His song about locusts singing for me.

They covered the ground and hung from branches
Those magical marvelous tree-faeries,
Flying around after shedding their shells,
Membranous wings translucent with veins of orange and gold.
Their sound was Earth's life force talking to me
Chirping Morse code messages sent by my dad.
The world was transfigured by this extraordinary wonder
Into a different place I got to inhabit
Where lost little boys lifted from grief
Believed in the possibility of impossible things.

Gender Crime

In a small house in New Jersey with nary a vine
Lived two little boys who rarely walked in straight lines
And sad they were without their dad,
These two brave, determined, dadless lads.
He'd died almost a year before
Leaving the boys on their own to learn and explore.
One day when the oldest was six, about to turn seven,
The big yellow bookmobile arrived on the street at
    half past eleven.
While he gathered books from the shelves in the carpeted wagon
The boy discovered *Madeline* by Ludwig Bemelmans.
He carried his books to the librarian's miniature desk
But she saw *Madeline* and for some reason found it grotesque
That a lad would select a book intended for a lass.
"This isn't for you!" the librarian said with a huff,
"Wouldn't you rather something about dinosaurs, cars or trucks?"
But Madeline lived in Paris in a fabulous house covered in vines
And the boy wanted to read how, in her stylish hat and cape,
    she spent her time.
He realized right away he had committed some crime
Filing away in his mind that a boy could be wrong about
    something he liked.
He was learning to think quite fast on his feet
Lying if it was necessary to get from adults what he needed.
The tale he spun for the librarian was simple and clean
Telling her his cousin, a girl, would be visiting that week
So he wanted a book she might like to read.
"What a thoughtful boy!" the librarian said with a smile
Never once considering his savvy smarts or capacity for guile.
The boy got the book he wanted to read
Making detailed brain notes he'd later remember to heed.
I'll figure this world out yet, the boy thought in his head,
Then he lay in the grass under a tall shady green tree

Shooing flying cicadas trying to land on his head, his arms, his
    knees
And read and re-read the story of Madeline,
A daring French girl who made lots of good trouble
With courage and joy and whimsy.

In the Surf at Asbury Park

I stand in the surf at Asbury Park,
A gangly eight-year-old wearing a white t-shirt to protect my pale
    skin from burning,
Water splashing my skinny legs as the waves roll in and out.
Two elderly men in sun hats sit on beach chairs under
    a nearby pier.
They get up and walk together toward the ocean holding hands.
What is this?
I've never seen two men holding hands before.
An airplane flies overhead with a sky banner for an
    amusement arcade,
Momentarily diverting my attention.
The plane flies south and I turn back to the men,
Watching them hold each other up as the water sprays their
    veiny, rickety legs.
They laugh at the splashing waves, just like we do.
Are my cousins and brother seeing this?
Aunt Mary, a tan raven-haired woman born on a farm in Ireland,
Gets up from under our green and red and
    yellow striped umbrella.
"Don't stare," she quietly says as she approaches,
 Not rounding us up and insisting we leave,
 Instead saying hello to the two men a short distance from
    us in the water.
"They're married," she whispers in her Irish brogue,
    "Like a man and a woman."
 Fascinated by the men, I keep staring despite Aunt Mary's
    admonition.
They reach down and scoop up seawater in their hands
Washing themselves with the salty ocean,
Then turn and walk back to their chairs
As we children continue to jump and play and scream
    in the waves.
One of the men stops to collect seashells from a tidal pool
    while the other supports him.

They examine the shells together.
This all seems important to me, though I don't know why.
The rhythmic roar of the crashing waves drowns my thoughts
As I return focus back to the endless ocean
And what appears to be a ship far off on the horizon.

Christmas Eve 1971

Earth spins and spins and spins
No matter what else is happening.
With my finger I could make it spin faster and faster
Trying to speed up time to get us further away
From September '69
When my father died.
Or I could make the planet spin the other way
Like Superman
Flying counter-rotationally to reverse time
So we might experience the sweetness of '68 again.

"It makes no sense," I said to my mother
As I spun the globe on its leaning axis.
I just didn't believe it possible for him to make the trip in one night.
You'd think I would have questioned first how reindeer could fly
But it was the timing logistics of the trip where I found holes
In this story they insisted on continuing to tell
A little boy who didn't care anymore
About fictions contrived to bring magic and glee.
"Don't tell your brother," my mother whispered to me
As she clawed still for happiness and normalcy.
"You're a big boy.
You're 8.
He isn't yet 6.
Tonight, you can stay up with me and help wrap the gifts."
Suddenly, I felt something resembling joy
Being now on the adult side of the tale
Complicit with my mother in creating delight for my brother.

Once he was asleep in the bed beside mine
My mother gently shook me when it was time,
Leading me to the living room — a room for the living —
Dark but for the twinkling lights of the tree
Illuminating our Irish setter Clancy
As he sniffed the presents already wrapped for me.

G.I. Joes and Tonka trucks and Matchbox cars waited in a pile
To be covered in red and green and silver and gold,
The Christmas morning loot for my brother
To temporarily alleviate our Christmas mourning for our father,
Who may or may not have hovered in spirit
Bouncing from twinkling light to twinkling light on the tree
Though still was not there,
Not in the way we needed him to be.
Our life was not a movie.
He never came bounding through the front door
Wearing a scarf
Dusted in snow
Clutching Zuzu's petals
Excited at the sheer experience of breathing,
His beating heart, by an angel, restored.

My Uncle's Gladiolas

At the tattered pink Tudor on Winding Way
My Uncle John keeps existence safe
Protecting everyone on Earth from tumbling into the afterlife,
A job inherited by our forebears in the West of Ireland
From Druids and witches
Who came before famine and strife.
Gladiolas surround the front yard between fresh-cut grass and hedge.
Shades of yellow, purple, orange, and red sway in the summer breeze
On stems resembling stalks almost as tall as me.
Strings attached to sticks support the more fragile blooms,
Giving form and shape to String Theory,
Explaining how there are dimensions beyond us standing in this yard.
I stare at the funnel-shaped flowers
Erupting along one side each of the green sword leaves
Certain they are staring back at me
Like extraterrestrial visitors who've taken root in Earth's soil.
A neighbor once called them death flowers,
Which seemed to amuse Uncle John and anger the gladiolas.
They stood up even straighter in the sunlight,
Strange alien creatures bursting defiantly with color
In the face of this accusation that they are entwined somehow with why we die.
If people place them in vases beside coffins
Maybe it's to ward off death, not embrace it.
I look at gladiolas differently now that I realize
They are centurions protecting one world from the other,
Marking the border between grass and hedge a demilitarized zone
Even though these flowers act as soldiers.
In the space over which they preside
Living and dead do not comingle.
We stay here and the departed stay there
Because it gets messy when worlds collide.

Gladiolas understand this and take seriously their guarding of the
> quantum border
Between Tir na nOg and New Jersey.
Maybe it's quite wonderful in the Otherworld
But we don't want people in a hurry to get from here to there
And no one really wants those gone
Coming back with spoilers for the Great Beyond.
I am only 10 years old
But comprehend there'd be chaos
Without gladiolas at the border.
That it comes down to one flower bed in New Jersey
Watched over by my gentle, offbeat uncle
Guarding all of creation,
Watering with a repurposed tomato paste can,
His pockets crammed with Wonder Bread for when we feed the ducks,
Makes perfect sense to me.
The place of my childhood is the center of the universe.
Every kid knows this about where they grow up.
I am fortunate to see gladiolas the way I do,
To live so close to the edge of being at such a young age and not
> be afraid.
When they retreat underground as winter approaches
Uncle John assures me they are still there
Beneath a layer of mulch insulation,
Vigilant sentries serving their sacred duty
Ensuring each human gets as long as is humanly possible
To live a human life
Before disappearing
Like my father
Into the dirt.

Sometimes She Still Comes to Me

Sometimes she still comes to me.
I made her up as a boy.
Marked by loss
I read a girl's diary
About a time and a place
Much much worse than my own,
Then I invented a girl
Like the one in the book
And asked her to live inside me.
When I was 6
After my father died
Before I invented the girl,
Alone in front of the television
I saw a movie about the camps,
Piles of corpses in black and white footage.
What is this?
I asked the television as my uncle would ask the spout.
Our downspout had become clogged,
Rainwater built up
Overflowing from the gutter.
Uncle Joe (I now know troubled by memories of war and liberating
    one of those camps)
Inspected with me by his side
Pulling out Little People
Made by Fisher-Price,
The blond-haired woman and the dog in the collar
The pig-tailed girl and the man in the hat
A dozen Little People clogging our spout.
Did you put these here?
My uncle softly asked.
I was hiding them
I tried to explain
As he handed me my Little People
To take into the woods so I could hide them there.
When I invented the girl

Several years later
I'd hide her inside me
Instead of the woods
Or up the spout.
Brown hair
Glasses
Her flowered 1940s dress,
She looked like a photograph of my mother taken during the war.
I would walk around outside in the world so she could see things,
Like jet planes and sparrows,
Other children playing in the park,
My marigold garden on the side of the house,
And keep me company
While I kept her safe.

Dancing Queen

The Bicentennial Minutes pass by
As my body changes,
As I change and turn 13
Alone in my room
With a new 45 of Abba's *Dancing Queen*
(*That's Me* on side B).
Holding the groovy vinyl disc
In my sweaty, busy pubescent hands,
I place it on the turntable
Ready to dance to the promised land.
My portable phonograph,
Orange, adorned in
Swirling
Trippy
Day-Glo
Daisies,
Plays Sonny & Cher,
Captain & Tennille,
The soundtrack from *A Chorus Line*,
And Sondheim's *Follies*.
The door closed tight
I fashion an outfit of billowing robes
Bedsheets and blankets suggesting royal gold
Fit for a queen
A dancing queen
Feel the beat from the tambourine.
A towel I wrap round my head
Make-believe bouncy seventies hair
Like Farrah Fawcett on the wall
Her red swimsuit poster my cover
For the boy who secretly calls.
I dance round that bedroom
Having the time of my life,
See that girl
Watch that scene

Dig the dancing queen
Terrified to be seen.
Exuberant and free
As I jump then twirl,
Knowing I am a boy
Not a girl,
But the wrong kind of boy
A camouflaged boy
Forced to hide in plain sight
Not show too much joy.
I learn how to be
What the world wants to see
Burying deep
The exuberant
Free
Tender
Me,
Determined no one mimic an unmanly limp wrist
Use the term fairy
Or call me she,
Though a radical faerie
A fierce dancing queen
An unburdened child
Is who I was meant to be.

The Nineteenth and Last Straight Boy I Loved

You were my friend
My straight boy friend
As in my friend who is a boy
Confiding in me about our mutual girl friend
As in our friend who is a girl.
You said to me over and over and over again
That you were in love with her.
I took on this role willingly,
Being your confidant,
Because I was in love with you
And this was how I thought you could need me.
I'd been in love like this before –
Secret love
Anguished love
Unrequited love.
In my Catholic schoolboy world, I was terrified to tell anyone what
    I felt about anything.
I suffered in silence for my sins
Even though they were not sins at all
Because now I know there is no such thing as sin.
I was sold this bill of nonsensical self-loathing
By every institution I thought I needed to survive.
Church, country, school
All turned out to be
Wrong
Wrong
Wrong.
Before I escaped from the darkness into the light
The world I believed I could not live without
Took a rusty carving knife to my body
Slicing me open from stem to stern
Snatching from my guts any capacity for joy that I had,
Which I thought was exactly what I deserved,
And left me to live life alone.
I was a gay Catholic boy

In a culture threatening and judgmental,
At the start of an epidemic decimating my people
Before I even knew who my people were.

But you?
I loved you.
I think more than I loved all the other dreamy straight boys
Of my undercover adolescence
I loved you.
Late one night during final exams you played the violin for me
In an empty moonlit classroom with six large windows
Bathing us in that midnight light fit for werewolves and vampires,
Dangerous creatures who would never view me as drenched in sin.
When you were done playing —
I recall Gershwin, then something soft, sweet you made up –
I wanted to touch you,
Feel your skin against mine.
And kiss you,
Kiss those satin lips that formed a luscious border around the
    mouth
From which your sultry voice came.
I looked into those dark bedroom eyes,
Heavy-lidded with a mischievous twinkle,
And ached to be naked with you.
That night I would have given up everything,
Which at that point was nothing,
To run away with you.
We would assume new identities
While living secretly somewhere together,
Perhaps a shack with chickens in the Florida Keys.
I had no role models,
No basis for believing I could be happy in an out-in-the-daylight-
    sort-of-way,

So even in my fantasies
We lived clandestine lives hidden from the world.
Yet despite the confusion
Despite the pain
Loving you was magic.
I think of the moonlit night you played violin for me over forty years ago.
I am there in that classroom with you again
Longing, aching
The decades melting
My heart melting.
I smile at the innocence
At the hopefulness
In which I loved you.
I love you. . . I love me,
Finally.

My Beautiful Passing Stranger

I remember one afternoon when I was 20
At the Bleecker Street Cinema
Disappearing myself into a double feature
Cleo from 5 to 7 and *Breathless,*
And breathless I was spit out
Into the bright glare and summer heat of 1983 New York City
After four air-conditioned hours in early '60s black-and-white Paris.
Feeling like a French New Wave extra
I roamed the winding warren of the West Village,
Disoriented every time I turned another corner.
As I passed Waverly on West 11th
Heading toward Seventh Avenue
Underneath a canopy of lush green trees
He approached
From the other direction
A handsome young stranger
Maybe 28
Who looked like Jean-Paul Belmondo
Dreamy with brown hair and brown eyes
Irresistibly sexy and cool
Like the character Michel leading Jean Seberg astray.
From a half block away
I could see his face, his neck
Covered in KS lesions,
A veil of blotches purple and brown.
I knew what it was
I knew about AIDS.
I was a barely-20-year-old closeted gay man
Who'd had unsafe sex.
I was terrified of AIDS.
We walked toward one another,
I ordered myself not to look away,
He got closer
I smiled at him
Our eyes locked

He returned the smile and nodded
I nodded back.
God, he was beautiful.
I fell in love.
Can you fall in love with a passing stranger?
The KS lesions were huge and everywhere.
I wanted to hold him
To ease his pain.
I understood my moral obligation
To see him and acknowledge him.
My humanity
His humanity
Demanded it.
We both turned for one last lingering glance.
I felt no pity
Though I thought I'd feel pity.
I felt drawn to him
Connected to him,
My dreamy Jean-Paul
What happened to him?
In my gut I doubt he survived.
Millions have passed me since him,
Some even nodded and smiled,
But he is the one
Who has remained with me.
He was
He is
He always will be
My
Beautiful
Passing
Stranger.

The Telegram and the Sea

I wasn't yet born
When the Western Union Telegram arrived,
Delivered to the white house on West End Avenue
By a man in a cap on a bike,
Who peddled the streets of Newark, New Jersey,
With his Deeply-Regret-To-Inform-You dispatches of death.
I wonder if each telegram had a heaviness to it
As it sat in the man's leather pouch?
Did he dread each delivery as he peddled along?
Or was he happy to be outside
Breezily riding the streets of Newark?
Don't shoot the messenger!
They always say,
Even if the messenger enjoys his work.

My grandmother Delia was home alone
As the man leaned his bike against the porch
Walked up the steps
Knocked on the door.
My mother Winnie arrived home from school,
Found Delia
Running from room to room
Gripping the telegram
Wailing
Pulling at her hair.
The Nazis shot down James' plane over the Adriatic Sea
During a bombing run in Yugoslavia of oil refineries.
Winnie took Delia in her arms,
A child cradling her mother.
Together they sobbed because James was dead.
Delia's son
Winnie's brother
Never coming home
They both knew as they sat entwined
Collapsed on the floor.

Newark 1944 faded into time,
Became Venice 1985,
41 years after the telegram arrived.
Salami, bread, cheese ripped apart with our hands,
A bottle of wine passed back and forth with a friend,
I marked turning 22 on the Lido di Venezia
Surrounded by pine trees and sand dunes across the lagoon.
I recalled James' story — A handsome rascal of a guy
With a deep longing for adventure,
A Clark Gable twinkle in his eyes.
I missed this man I never met during my life
And ached to touch him any way that I could.
The blue water of the Adriatic –
Low in ammonia
Low in nitrates
Reflecting the light –
Is clearer, brighter than a starry night.
Swimming in the Adriatic
My eyes open wide
Allowed me to see forever in that sea
Of lost planes and family lore,
See out for miles and miles
Back to the war in '44.

I held my breath and dove in
Kicking my legs to propel me forward,
Finding James in the aquatic flora and fauna
Part of the algae and marine life.
That beautiful man long ago decomposed,
Dissolved into water
I took in through my mouth, my eyes, my nose.
I took him into me
A communion
One old altar boy to another,

And stayed down with James in his watery grave
So long as my breath allowed,
Holding my breath a little bit longer
Fighting the urge to rise
Knowing my breath was the portal
To that night when James lost his life.
I wanted to hold my breath forever
But I couldn't, no one can.
I shot up through the water in a torrent of bubbles
Back to the surface in 1985, an exhausted and gratified man.
I finished something that day
In the northern basin of the Adriatic
For my mother, my grandmother, myself, and James
That began decades ago
Before I was alive
At the old white house on West End Avenue
When the Western Union Telegram arrived.

Fuck the Nazis

I saw him at the barbed wire fence
Then near the crematorium
And by the wall outside
Covered in creeping ivy
Where they shot people
Where they shot gay men
Imprisoned by Paragraph 175,
Downward-pointing pink triangles
Collapsing to the ground
With the butchered men wearing them.
I noticed him touching the bullet holes
Still there in 1985,
Tracing them with his finger.
I walked away
Left him to trace
Walked alone down corridors of barracks
No longer there.
Inside a museum I came upon giant photos
Not from Dachau,
Auschwitz, I believe.
Hungarian Jewish women
Hungarian Jewish children
About to be murdered.
A child's American voice
Over and over echoed
From somewhere in the museum
But Mommy
Why did they kill the children?
Why did they kill the children?
Why did they kill the children?
Inside my head I screamed
Goddamn it, answer her!
Make her stop asking.
And tell me, too,
Why did they kill the children?

Why did they kill anyone?
A mother's voice finally replied,
The bad people who killed the children were gone.
He'd appeared again.
I looked at him while the mother spoke
He looked at me
We both knew
The bad people weren't gone.
The child asked one more thing,
Once the bad people were gone
Did the children come back to life?
No answer followed.
Palpable sorrow hung in the air.
In front of a woman
Hunched over with children
Her children
Four of them
Barefoot
In rags,
Jews from Carpatho-Ruthenia
On their way to the gas chamber
It said underneath the photo,
He slumped to the floor
And covered his face.
I walked away.

On the train back to Munich
Crowded with Germans
There he was
Coming toward me
Down the aisle
Brown hair
Tan skin
Translucent green eyes.
Please sit down, I thought.

He did.
We talked
We flirted.
What is wrong with me?
Went the voice in my head
This is the train from Dachau.
His arm grazed mine
It lingered,
Ben
Sweet Ben
His name was Ben,
They killed gay men
At Dachau,
Fuck the Nazis
I let our arms graze again.
We were in Germany
Ben was from Haifa
The closet
My closet
My large walk-in American closet
Did not hold me that day.
I told myself no one at home would know.
In Munich we walked
And talked
And walked
And talked
About the war
About the camp.
On a street corner he kissed me
In the bright summer daylight
Germans everywhere seeing us kiss,
It felt like liberation.
"Come to my room," Ben said.
I went.
We fucked
Fuck the Nazis

All afternoon we fucked
Fuck the Nazis
A Gay Jew fucking an American Queer
Fuck the Nazis
We won
Fuck the Nazis
We fucked
Fuck the Nazis
Our triumph
Fuck the Nazis
Ben said it while we fucked
Fuck the Nazis
Then I said it
Fuck the Nazis
Fucking as revenge
Fuck the Nazis
Revenge fucking
Fuck the Nazis
It felt good
Fuck the Nazis
Really good
Fuck the Nazis
I think we fucked 175 times
Fuck the Nazis
In their Bavarian city Munich
Beer Hall Putsch Munich
The Sudetenland handed over by Chamberlain there Munich
Fuck the Nazis.
We never met again
Ben and I
But we'll always have Munich.
Fuck the Nazis
Fuck
Fuck
Fuck
Fuck the Nazis.

The Gathering of Magical Children

I have only begun to unravel my secret,
Revealing who I am to the world.
Many years ago
Magical children in great danger were hidden
Everywhere in plain sight.
Dark forces intent on their destruction searched the earth
So sanctuaries were found,
Safe places where time could pass until the threat died down.
I caught glimpses throughout my life
Of belonging to something bigger
And different than the world I knew.
Slowly, as revelation and transformation occurred
Connections were made among the magical children.
Community was built.
It did not come easy, this unraveling and revealing of who we really are.
There were moments of dancing on summer nights
Amidst the fireflies and faeries
But there were days of monsters and maelstroms, too.

When you hide magical children
Without properly recording where they are hidden
You leave it to the children themselves to crawl
From their caves and hovels and hollowed-out trees,
Which takes years and years and years,
Trust me.
Many of the hidden children will never be found
Though how many we cannot know
Because as I said, the recording of where the magical children were hidden
Was done haphazard at best
And those that did the hiding are long gone
Leaving each of us alone to our quest.
I don't resent that I was hidden
As I emerge into the light.

The hiding is over.
I am leaving what was lost and cannot be changed
Firmly
In the past.

ACTing UP in The Milky Way

Army of brothers
Army of sisters
Sister-brothers
Brother-sisters
ACTing UP
Fighting back
Leading me to liberation
From my twentysomething closet
Where I hid from AIDS
Hid from homophobia
Hid from myself.
Thought I was keeping the monsters at bay
But only kept jubilation at bay
During those dark Ronald Reagan mean ugly days.
We were
We are
A diverse
Non-partisan
Group of individuals
United in anger
And committed to direct action
To end the AIDS crisis,
Said the facilitator
At the start of every meeting.
In the winter of '89
ACT UP stormed a church
That had welcomed them not
And I marched my younger gay self
To the L and the G
Not yet a B and a T
Let alone a Q and an I
Community Center
Inside a ramshackle old school on West 13th
Where I found my people
Fighting my fight,

Screaming
Planning
Demanding
An end to the nightmare called AIDS,
Cracking open my heart
To let in the light,
Replacing fear
With the priceless gift
Of knowing who I am
Of loving who I am.
My first Monday Night Meeting was electrically charged
Fierce women
Hot men
Hot women
Fierce men
Rollerena dressed as a fairy godmother
Gliding through the room with the rent pumpkin.
I enlisted as a foot soldier
At the age of 26
In this war declared against us
As if it was 1941,
Because make no mistake
There were all kinds of fascists again
Wanting us dead
Wanting us erased from public life,
Ignoring the cries of young gay men
Beautiful men
Talented men
Funny men
Smart men
Brave men
Kind men
Resilient men
Outrageous men
Who would never know 30 or 40 or 50.

Women, straight men, children died, too,
Casualties as well of the Gay Plague
As it was called in the papers and on the evening news.
Twice a week I held some of those children in Washington Heights,
Sitting with them on my lap
Gently patting their backs
While a nebulizer delivered medication to their lungs –
Their tiny, vulnerable, infected lungs –
Aware these children might never know 3 or 4 or 5.

Unconcerned with all this suffering,
They gathered faggots to place round the stakes
Those Bible-thumping American fascists,
Carrying torches to set the faggots ablaze.
But the faggots fought back.
The dykes did, too,
Avenging lesbians unafraid of fire.
I recall trans pioneers there as well
Facing oppression outside and inside the room
Recognizing our communal situation as dire.
Together these queers
Started a revolution
Toppled institutions
Transformed a community
Saved millions of lives
Saved my life
From fear and despair and the belief
That this disease would eventually take me, too.
There was little hope
And even less joy
Before ACT UP
For men like me
Who were told
Time and time again

Throughout our lives
That we did not matter
That we deserved to die
Because of whom we loved and how we lived,
Which wasn't that different, really,
From how everyone lives.
Holding on to a promise
Made to us as children
That life would reveal
Wonder and magic
And it would be ours
To enjoy and devour
All the days and all the nights
We roamed this spinning planet,
Located on a reaching twisting arm
27,000 light-years from the center of a galaxy
Named by the Romans
Road Made of Milk,
Surrounded by billions upon billions upon billions
Of
Fading
Brilliant
Shooting
Stars,
Luminous balls of hydrogen and helium
Hanging in the heavens,
Their light only reaching us
Long after they're actually
Permanently
Gone.

Baptism on the Broadway-Seventh Avenue Local

Bodies, backpacks, bulky coats
Arms reaching from every direction
Trying to find a surface to grab
Something to hold onto that is not another person
While somewhere in the crowd someone violently coughs.
Winter evening rush hour on the 1 train.
The New York City subway is the great equalizer for $1.15,
A small metal token the size of a dime
And I can commune with all the world
Trapped together
In one closed claustrophobic space
Hurtling underneath the city
From Coney Island to the Cloisters.
Then I spot her amidst the arms and heads and torsos,
Her sporty gray page cut giving her away.
I muster the courage and approach
Clearing a path through the intertwined cranky New Yorkers.
"Excuse me," I say, "Were you leading the ACT UP meeting last
    night?"
A big smile and eyes filled with curiosity greet me.
"Yes, that was me."
"It was my first time at an ACT UP meeting," I disclose.
"My first time ever in the Lesbian and Gay Community Center."
"I'm Ann Northrop. What did you think?"
"It was amazing. You were incredible."
"I hope you'll come back again," she warmly says.
"Absolutely," I reply as she removes the Silence = Death button
    from her lapel,
 Pinning the button on me
In the middle of so much humanity.
"Welcome to the fight," she says,
 Baptizing me a queer AIDS activist
 On the Broadway-Seventh Avenue Local,

Making me think of *Casablanca*
Victor Laszlo and Rick standing on the rainy, foggy airport tarmac
Laszlo welcoming Rick to the fight
Shaking his hand
Predicting
Promising
"This time I know our side will win."
A crowded subway car was my rainy, foggy tarmac,
Silence = Death printed on a metal button
Underneath a pink triangle
Given to me by Ann Northrop
My call to the fight.

Sullivan Street

Hitchcock's *The Birds* was playing on television
In the Sullivan Street fourth-floor walk-up
Just south of Houston
That sunny Saturday morning I arrived
Clutching a list of names and addresses from the Gay Roommate Service
And met Craig.
We got to know each other as gulls and sparrows and crows attacked poor Tippi Hedren,
Leaving her blond updo disheveled
Her green wool suit ruined.
I knew I was home.
Departing Jersey for Manhattan overwhelmed me like a latter-day Mary Ann Singleton,
But I acclimated to living at the center of the universe.
Our building was filled with sweet ancient Italian women
All approaching 100 then
All long gone now.
The apartment's windows,
Screenless and wide open,
Never posed a danger.
No mosquito or bird or burglar ever came inside,
Just a series of neighborhood cats I would sometimes find curled up on my bed
And once a giant weird stick bug in the corner that looked extraterrestrial.
My bedroom belonged in the 1950s to Charles Nelson Reilly of 1970s *Match Game* fame
Said the sweet ancient Italian women.
Did Charles ever come home to find a weird skinny stick alien in the corner?
Each June I would look out my bedroom window
The one with the fire escape
And watch the Ferris wheel of the St. Anthony Feast
Spin round and round with people staring in at me,

Strangely sometimes waving as if I was part of the ride.
Then the night of February 26, 1993,
I climbed out on the fire escape with Craig,
Shocked to see only one World Trade Center tower lit
Like the other tower had disappeared.

I remember the early 1990s as if they were the late 1960s,
A liberating, exhilarating, debauched four years.
Sullivan Street was gay college.
We drank too much Tequila
Smoked too many cigarettes
Had lots of sex (safe and not with each other)
And stayed out way too late way too often,
Racing the rats home at dawn from the East Village.
We met for coffee at Life Café
Celebrated birthdays at Universal Grill
Danced at Crow Bar and Wonder Bar
Protested and went to ACT UP meetings every Monday night.
I recall squeezing into our pocket-sized bathroom with
    Jamie Bauer and Alexis Danzig
Like we were reenacting the Marx Brothers' stateroom scene from
    A Night at the Opera,
Mixing wheatpaste in the shower for a night of
    ACT UP-wheatpasting across SoHo.
I remember filming talk shows with the camcorder in our
    living room,
Which was also the kitchen,
Inviting our friends to pop by the apartment as guests,
Long before Kramer did it on *Seinfeld*.
R.E.M., ABBA, Eurythmics, The Smiths, early Madonna mixed
    with
St. Anthony's church bells,
Traffic on Houston Street,
The neighbors fighting (turned out to be rehearsal of a play),
And Craig's revered Carpenters

As Sullivan Street's score and soundtrack.
There was this hopeful optimism of knowing we've only just begun,
And not just on rainy days and Mondays.
We were mischievous, unbound twentysomethings
Indulging ourselves a libertine freedom neither could have imagined
While living as isolated gay boys in postmodern America.
That I was given Sullivan Street at all meant somewhere in my youth or childhood,
I must have done something good.

Just Before the Cocktails Came

It was unexpected to find myself young during a time of war
When the bombs fell selectively, precisely,
And strangers sitting near me on the subway knew nothing at all.
There were two cities then, AIDStown and New York.
A person lived in one place or the other,
Two universes running parallel within the same world at once.

We met as the eighties wound down,
You all muscles and sarcasm and impatience underneath a mop of
    punkish blond hair.
We'd both found our way to ACT UP and jokingly calling it
    ACT UP High,
The queer teenage experience we finally got to have
If high school had been the French Resistance
Taking on the Great Bubonic Pestilence.

You were a sexy cool kid,
Bartender, musician, Rock N Roll Fag Bar star.
I was less cool, tentative, wandering in and out of
    ACT UP meetings,
Lingering at the edge of protests.
I was an alley cat raised by wolves sniffing trash cans in the alley
    for the first time,
A little afraid, a lot excited, by finding finally the alley and the cans.

The end came sooner than we planned.
I remember how your skin felt when I last touched your hand,
Paper-thin and willowy like an old man.
You'd moved to San Francisco, so I hadn't seen you in months.
As I approached the corner of Ashbury and Haight you stood
    there smiling, leaning on a cane,
Having gone from muscly to emaciated in the span of one winter
    and two weeks of that spring.

It happened back then before the good drugs came.
1993, 1994, 1995 — guys our age still died in droves
Disappearing from Chelsea, the Village, Cherry Grove.
Not like the early days when no one knew anything, and
    everyone was in shock
But a dying on the eve of salvation when the cocktails came out,
Highly active antiretroviral therapies that would save millions of
    lives.

You missed it. Just missed it. We had no idea then how close we
    were to that,
Still in the Dying Years when you accepted your looming death
    and rehomed Godzilla, your cat.
As you slipped in and out of consciousness, unable to stay,
Your beautiful body ravaged by AIDS, the pandemic that ravaged
    our gay salad days,
You asked of me one thing, dear Howard my friend,
To write about you, not leave you lost in the fray.

Annie Lennox Singing

Sitting on a Formica kitchen chair
At a breezy backyard picnic
On the hilly outskirts of the Castro
San Francisco 1997
Late afternoon springtime
California lilacs blooming
Bright light streaming
Through the branches of a bay laurel,
Annie Lennox singing
From a hidden CD player
Perched behind the window screen,
Looking at the long-distance man I love
Who may or may not love me back,
His graying hair touched by the golden-hour beams
His soft skin warm compared to the breeze
As my arm brushes his,
Another blissful tale of the city.
It's not like watching something real
Even as it's happening
But more like watching film footage,
Old home movies
The images jumping
Clicking and blinking,
Not the present at all
But like it all really happened thirty years ago.

Any given moment,
Which is all we ever have
And all we ever are,
The place where we are supposed to ground ourselves,
Is less than fleeting
Lacking even the permanence of ephemeral experience
Already over as we are just beginning to savor it,
Not even trying to hold onto it
Wanting only to brush against it

Feel its warm skin,
Hopefully taste it
Our teeth biting into its flesh
Like an overstimulated cat
Drinking the blood of beauty and joy.
It is ours for less than a zeptosecond
The shortest measure of time recorded
One trillionth of a billionth of a second,
Barely perceptible to our human brains
But all that our souls perceive and understand.
We film these home movies
To sustain us in our later years,
Turning the projector on inside our heads
When there is more time behind us than ahead of us,
Watching these younger days again in our gloaming
Content to face the night.

Little Red Cabin on the Hill

At the confluence of two creeks, the Esopus and Stony Clove,
Hid a hamlet called Phoenicia.
On a hill outside town sat a little red cabin
Made of wood and stone and memory and greasepaint,
The forest nearby sheltering deer, chipmunk, woodland pixies.
Built in 1911, nails were being hammered, the cabin coming to life,
As three hours away near Washington Square Park
The Triangle Shirtwaist Factory Fire seared one more scar into the
    psyche of a city.
Alighting from Adirondacks Trailways
Onto Main Street Phoenicia
Surrounded by mountains
The decades peeled back
Leaving me a time traveler in a languorous world without
    television or cell phones.
Greeting me as I disembarked the bus always was Stephen.
While the cabin was built in 1911,
Stephen was built during the war.
Having performed on Broadway
Rioted at Stonewall
Gossiped with Bacall,
A trail of midcentury history and pixie dust followed us as we
    strolled to Sweet Sue's,
Then made our way after pancakes out of town up the hill to the
    little red cabin.

Peggy Lee sang from the CD player,
Her voice caressing the warm Catskills summer air
As we indulged a toke sitting on the porch-swing
Sinking into the mountains and trees and dragonflies,
Siamese cats rubbing against our legs
Ozzzy in particular climbing up to park himself in my lap.
A world-class raconteur, I devoured Stephen's stories
Like the sweet summer corn from Alice and Roger's stand
    up the road.

"Tell me again about hanging with Garland," I said
As we planted flowers at the side of the cabin we hoped the deer wouldn't eat.
Back on the front porch,
Sunflowers from town in one vase
Wildflowers from the meadow in another,
We read and ate enormous blueberries from a vintage yellow enamelware bowl
While spirits gathered and frolicked in the yard
Mixing with the hummingbirds, butterflies and bees.
Danny visited often, coming down the stairs, sitting with us on the porch.
Howard, my introduction to Stephen, lingered late every evening until we went to bed.

The ghosts of gone gay men drifted everywhere then
And the little red cabin on the hill was no exception.
Up on that hill and out in the world, we survivors walked like displaced persons.
But oh, how we also danced and laughed in the uncut meadow.
We men of such loss managed astonishing feats of happiness
And dove to depths of great joy,
Eternal brothers
Holding each other
Leading each other
Together toward a new century.
Thank you Phoenicia and Esopus Creek
Thank you mountains and sky
Thank you little red cabin on the hill
Surrounded by starlight and magic and fireflies.
Once again, somewhere in my youth or childhood. . .

The Flyers

First a trickle
Then a deluge,
On community bulletin boards and storefronts
Lampposts and subway signs
Chain-link fences and cement barricades
Church walls and shop windows
Bus stops and *Village Voice* distribution boxes,
The flyers began to appear
After they disappeared,
Secretaries from Kew Gardens
Investment bankers from TriBeCa
Cops from Staten Island
Receptionists from Yonkers
Dishwashers from Jersey City
Waiters from Harlem
Insurance adjusters from Brooklyn Heights
Janitors from the Bronx
Firefighters from the Rockaways
Lawyers from the Upper East Side
Mailroom clerks from Newark.
We got to know their faces, their names, their ages,
Where they worked
Which tower they had been in
What floor they had been on
The clothing they wore to work that day.
Held up with staples and tape
They remained flapping in the breeze
As the days turned into weeks
The nights grew cooler
The leaves started to fall
And the air stopped tasting
Like metal, glass, jet fuel, vaporized office equipment, death.
Time had stopped when the buildings came down
And the flyers went up.
We lived with them until we no longer did,

Still finding one now and then
Balled up in the gutter or wedged under a bench,
Opening and flattening it reverentially,
As 2001 ended
And 2002 began.

The Sky of Another Planet

Standing on the south rim of the Grand Canyon at sundown
I feel like I'm looking out on Mars,
The red and orange carved-out craters jutting into one another
Jutting and rolling
Limestone, sandstone, shale
Ancient and undisturbed
Exceeding all expectation.
Hues of yellow across the horizon
Turn to amber and poppy
Salmon and indigo
Mulberry, heliotrope and orchid.
We love sunsets because they subconsciously remind us of the sky
    of another planet,
That place we don't remember
Our Krypton
From whence we were jettisoned
Before crashing into Earth.
It was quite violent
How we each came shooting into the atmosphere
Like comets blazing fiery trails,
A traumatic start to this human adventure.
No wonder we lead lives of isolated angst
Given where we come from
And how we got here,
Thinking we are alone
In this strange sensation of not belonging.
We don't know that we miss the red and pink and purple sky
    of home
But we do ache for it
And search for it
Standing before it with our mouths open when it appears,
Trying to capture on our cameras the colors exploding
Because as we look at it
We find ourselves
Wanting to hold onto the intangible feeling

Of melancholy longing
For a place we never knew
That calms our disquiet
And makes us somehow complete.

Do You Believe in Magic? (July 2007)

The road reaches out before us along the Florida Straits
Dividing the ocean and the gulf
Like your languid arm
As you recline against it in the grass on a hot summer day.
In the car with the top down
Because all the rental place had left was a convertible
You put the Lovin' Spoonful in the CD player
While I try to dodge the speed traps as we sail over water,
Our hair blowing wild
Salt wafting up into our noses
Reminding us both of childhood seaside excursions.
We don't talk as we drive
Since it's easy for us to be together in silence
Listening to the Lovin' Spoonful,
And it's magic, if the music is groovy
It makes you feel happy like an old-time movie.
Key Largo
That's the movie,
Always a treat when it appears on TCM
As we enjoy our evening martinis.
Bogie
Bacall
Claire Trevor singing off-key for a drink
Winning her Oscar.
I've never felt freer than cruising U.S. Route 1 with you,
Thinking about the bus in the opening scene
Riding the same stretch of highway
Bringing Bogart to Bacall.
Blue water surrounds us like the blues from a Matisse painting,
Cerulean swirling into turquoise and ultramarine.
Palm trees dot the 2000 tiny limestone islands,
Some of which we drive across without ever knowing we've
    been there
Because that's how tiny I mean by tiny.
They're the remnants of ancient coral reefs and sand bars

That flourished 125,000 years ago,
And they'll probably be submerged under water by the eighties.
Not our eighties, our fabulous eighties,
But the 2080s
The doomsday
Climate change
Everyone-better-learn-how-to-swim-by-then eighties.
Still, that's more than seventy years away,
By then I'll be gone
You'll be gone
Certainly, this convertible will long be gone.
People should do something about that,
About the islands sinking
The oceans rising,
But they won't
Not really,
Not the way they'd need to so that 2000 tiny islands are saved.
It's science
Not magic
That will save these beautiful, damned coral atolls.
Do you believe in science?
That's what I should have called this poem.
I'll tell you about the science
And it'll free your soul
But it's like trying to tell a stranger 'bout rock and roll.

The Last Metro

I walked into Richard's studio as he pinned a canvas to the wall,
An enormous canvas I could have wrapped around me like a
  blanket.
I saw the red paint, the brushes lined up ready to go.
Edith Piaf sang from the CD player splattered in acrylic and oil.
She sang for the German occupiers, too,
While working for the Resistance,
A complicated life in a complicated time.
We'd cancelled Coco Chanel
But couldn't bring ourselves to cancel Piaf.
Her resistance cancelled her collaboration we said.
Richard was a boy during the war
Sprawled out on the floor with his comic books
In front of the radio
Listening to Fibber McGee and Molly
Edgar Bergen and Charlie McCarthy
The Shadow and Flash Gordon
Churchill and FDR.
He remembered Eleanor's broadcasts, too.

Richard stared at the blank canvas as I settled into a chair,
The shaky French Provincial one splattered also with paint.
Then the symphony began
Not from the CD player,
Piaf still sang,
A silent symphony conducted by Richard's hands
As red paint flew onto the canvas
Dripping down
Onto the floor
Bleeding everywhere
No way to stop the blood once Richard began
A river of blood flowing out the door, down the stairs,
  onto Broadway.

The night before we'd watched *The Last Metro* on TCM.
Richard said that was the painting's name
Even before the paint began to fly.
"It's Occupied Paris," he said, switching brushes.
More red paint
More blood dripping
The blood of occupation
The blood of the Vel' d'Hiv' Roundup
The blood of Drancy
The blood of trains heading east.
To have a front row seat as an artist turns paint into blood,
A transformation
A transubstantiation,
Is a transcendent experience.
Did someone sit and watch Picasso paint *Guernica*
Or Goya paint *The Third of May, 1808*
Witnessing the conception, gestation and birth of those paintings
As I witnessed *The Last Metro* come to life
And drip blood onto the gray wooden floor?

Little Man

When I was 6 years old, they called me little man of the house
As if that would comfort me
Not freak me out
Informing me I was responsible
For my mother, my brother, the world, myself.
I try to parent that little boy from here
What remains of him inside me
Telling him nothing was his fault
Nothing was his responsibility
He only needs to play and heal.
But he isn't sure what it means to heal
So despite the difficulty
I travel back to him in time
Arriving on a winter's day
When the air is frigid cold
Snow falling
The smell of 1970s in the air —
Naugahyde and Elmer's glue
Cigarette smoke and warm Tollhouse cookies
Childhood loss and wet dog fur.
I put my head back, open my mouth, let snowflakes fall on
    my tongue.
Tastes like winter of '72 snow.
I walk down the road to our house
My heart stopping when I spot through the picture window
    my mother
Her hair jet black and shoulder length again.
I don't knock on the door
Since I look too much like my father
And wish not to frighten or confuse her.
Besides, I am not here for my mother.
I continue past the house up the hill and wait for him.
He emerges from the back door, bundled in a snowsuit,
An Irish setter following as he trudges through our snowy yard to
    the woods.

The dog spots me and off he runs
Somehow knowing
Not at all confused by the metaphysical conundrum.
Clancy jumps up
Reaches his paws around my waist
Licks my cold face with wild abandon.
"Good boy. My good boy. My good, good boy. I've missed you," I say.
He comes chasing Clancy,
Sees me, stops and speaks,
"He usually doesn't run to strangers."
"Is that a snow fort you're building there in the woods?" I ask.
"I don't talk to strangers, too."
"And you never should."
"Do I know you?" he asks. "You remind me of my father."
"People tell me that. I knew your dad."
The snow falls harder as I continue
Saying things that need to be said
But weren't said then by anyone.
"Your snow fort looks awesome. Even from over here."
"Thanks," he replies, smiling, looking back toward his fort.
"Also, I want to say nothing was your fault. You're an incredible boy."
"Are you an angel?" he asks.
"An angel, yes, sorta. . . I gotta go. Just know nothing was your fault. Including your dad dying. He loves you very much. He is so proud of you."
The boy flings himself at me
Wraps his thin arms around my legs
Presses his face into my stomach.
I take off his hat
Kiss him on top of the head
Smelling his unwashed blond hair.
"Go back and finish building your fort," I say.
Loving this boy more than I've ever loved another child
Feeling my love for him course through my veins

Wanting to protect him
From everything awful he will face
All of which I know.
"Other than me, yes, never talk to strangers. None of the rest will be angels."
The boy nods and promises.
"I'll come back again and see you if I can," I say.
He takes off into the woods
Stops once, turns around, waves.
I return the wave,
My sweet little boy
You're going to be a man one day
Who travels back as I have done.
Then I watch him trek with determination to finish our fort,
Clancy frolicking behind crunching his paws against the snow,
The afternoon winter light through the leafless trees receding
As the particles in my hands begin to dissolve
And slowly I disappear
Back to the future,
Because people come and go so quickly here.

Little Men

Two little boys play together on the floor.
Solid beech wood blocks spread chaotically around them become
    a castle,
On second thought a skyscraper,
Actually, a fort.
Two grown men sit near the playing boys
Entranced by their wee hands reaching for more blocks
To make the castle-skyscraper-fort higher and higher
Until inevitable collapse followed by screams and infectious giggles.
"That was us," one man whispers to the other. "We were these ages
    when Dad died."
The other man sighs and nods with acknowledgment,
Finally getting it
Understanding who he was
Who his brother was
Because he can see it in his nephews as they rebuild their fort.
These two boys — only 6 and 4 — would be devastated to lose
    their father.
This is the enormity of the loss experienced decades ago by the
    two grown men,
Something they denied until it was recreated for them
By the boys and the wooden blocks,
Staring them in the face so they could no longer pretend
All is fine
They are fine
Really, everything is fine
There's nothing to see here
Just two semi-orphaned boys
Forced to become men
Alone
On their own
Without a road map
Without a guide.
But here's the thing —
The two little boys healed the two grown men,

Helping them to understand
What exactly took place
On that mid-September day
So long ago
When no one yet wrote 1970 on their checks
And the Vietnam War raged
Across Richard Nixon's America.

Beside a Death Bed (August 2010)

One Breath... Two Breaths... Three Breaths...
Counting the breaths
Each hard fought
During four days of morphine coma.
"Let go," I whisper into your ear.
"You don't have to remain here."
But you fight so hard to stay.
Four days earlier
Before you lost consciousness
You beckoned me closer
Kissed me on the mouth
Said, "I love you."
I am 47
Not 6 this time,
You are 85.
Losing a parent now is different
I understand what is happening
Things can be said.
"I love you," I replied.

The day before our final words
Your room was crowded with spirits,
So you told us,
Though you didn't refer to them as spirits.
You were gathering your angels.
"Flo's here."
"Ma... She's sitting in that chair."
"Ginger, good girl... My sweet Ginger."
It made me happy the dogs showed up, too,
Which reminded me I promised you
The ashes of both dogs
Clancy and Ginger
Would go in the coffin at your feet.
I must go home and find those ashes.
My other promise

Take Barnaby to live with me
I'll also keep,
Becoming a cat person
While I look after that gentle old black cat,
Giving him a great third act
As I care for the remaining piece of you,
Ultimately holding Barnaby in my arms three years hence
When he dies in the back seat of a cab on our way to the vet,
A quintessential New York City death.

We all take turns sitting by the bedside
These last days of Winnie
Knowing they are last days
Trying to talk you through to the other side
Whispering in your ear those things we think you need to hear
To leave your tired body
And soar out the window
Over New Jersey
Up
Up
Up
Through the troposphere
The stratosphere
The mesosphere
The thermosphere
The exosphere
Leaving all the fear
Leaving us
Because it's time
For you.
It's time
For whatever comes next.

Ode to an Art Studio

In this life we are lucky
To find places of magic and joy
That fulfill the childhood promises
Made to us by fairy tales,
But magical places are fleeting I know.
An enchanted art studio
Born in the 20th century
Enduring in the 21st
Was such a space existing out of time,
1920s Paris mixed with 1950s New York City,
As if Jackson Pollock visited Gertrude Stein's salon.
I first walked into Richard's atelier in January 2004
At the top of the old Broadway Studio Building constructed
    in 1905,
Bathed in winter light from two enormous skylights
    northern-exposed.
For forty years this was Richard's home,
Cluttered with art supplies
And artwork
And the detritus everywhere of an artist's life well-lived.
The smell of paint, gesso, turpentine, aerosol adhesive fix-it
    lingered in the air.
Maria Callas, Billie Holiday, Etta James, Joni Mitchell, Chet Baker
Took turns singing from a CD player splattered in paint,
Their voices blending with jack hammers and car horns and
    delivery trucks below
As the collages and murals and drawings
Leapt out of Richard's hands and mind.
Saturday afternoons from the radio
The opera — always the opera — filled the room.
Giant canvases with torn uneven edges
Hung from the walls
Like animal skins after a hunt,
Every color of paint imaginable dripping onto the
    gray wooden floor.

The studio was Richard's sanctuary, his fortress, his nest, his cave.
When he died
It was where I went to be with him
Even though he was no longer there
Because that's exactly where Richard remained
For a time
For me.

I Did Not Know How Hard It Would Be

I did not know how hard it would be when you died.
Twelve years, you and I — fourteen percent of my life if I live to
    be eighty-five –
All of them infused with an intensity of living
That only the intensity of a person
Who dares create art for a living
Can bring to the table,
A table cluttered with half-empty tubes of paint and brushes and
    paper cut-outs
Waiting to become a collage.
You were scattered in your thoughts and overwhelmed by how
    difficult things turn
No matter how much we set our minds to things not turning
    difficult,
Which strangely made life easier for me because I had one job,
To calm your thoughts and buck you up as you trudged through
    your seventh
And then eighth decades
Turning those paper cut-outs and paint into works of art
That people hung on their walls
And look at still everyday
As they struggle along themselves.
When you died,
And I no longer had to keep you going while you were well
Or nurse you while you were sick,
I had just the cat to talk to about this person who was always there
Now was nowhere anywhere in our lives
Except maybe lingering between the columns of ether
That line the hall between this world and the next.
I don't know what happens when we die.
While you were still alive, I went to a medium,
An ex-nun with a Buster Brown haircut named Janet,
And my mother came through during the reading,
Causing you to promise me that when you died
You would find a way to talk to me.

This left me hunting for messages everywhere
As I endured your disappearance,
Coming home to tell the cat how you revealed yourself
   to me that day.
I am smart and know this proves nothing
About what happens to us when we die.
But the cat agreed with me that your absence was so painful for us
It opened a portal using our pain as the key.
In fact, it was the cat's idea to devote myself to the seeking of your
   ethereal presence
Throughout this mean hard-around-the-edges world we were left
   to navigate
Without you ever again walking in or out the door.
When you died, I realized I'd forgotten what life is like when I'm
   alone making decisions
Minus that buffer of doing things for you,
Which always made me less afraid
Because it was part of my job in caring for you
To vanquish all monsters, setbacks, uncertainty, and fear.
But it was your intensity that propelled us forward I know now,
So naturally I slowed down a bit once you were gone,
Gently leading myself back from the shadowy shore of sorrow
By understanding why you loved me so much.
See, you didn't just love me.
You brought me to understand
Why I deserved to be loved like that.

Crosswalk

I wait for the light to change
Then enter the intersection
Moving slowly in the heat,
Halfway across I don't think I can finish the journey.
I stop
The traffic idles there
Assuming I will continue
Once the light changes again.
But my grief has hit me
In the middle of the crosswalk,
It shows up like this
Out of the blue,
My limbs won't do their job and carry me forward.
Can't I lie down here in the middle of the street?
The invisible people show up again
Moving my legs for me.
I make it across
Anchor myself to the sidewalk.
An old man passing looks at my face
He seems momentarily shocked by my despair,
Then the breath of recognition
Ah, loss, his soul whispers to mine
As all the souls strolling by peer out from their human bodies
And nod with understanding
At my loneliness
And
Steadfast
Sorrow.

I Know I'm Watching This from There

I know I'm watching this from there
As I endeavor to make the best of things
Even though my insides have been yanked out of my gut,
Dragging on the ground alongside me as I walk down the street.
I am a disemboweled mess
But the sunlight is hitting my face at an exquisite angle
While a host of sparrows hop from branch to branch in some
    nearby bramble.
This is no stiff-upper-lip bullshit.
I am on a soul mission to experience joy despite the pain.
My insides are always going to hang a little bit on the outside of
    my body,
So I can't wait until they are neatly coiled up
Resting inside my stomach
For the beauty of New York City on an early spring day to be savored.
I need to marvel at the crocuses now
As if no one has ever seen them before,
Really be with the crocuses
Instead of already anticipating the daffodils
Or longing for the tulips.
When I said I'm watching this from there
I meant that it is all transitory — the pain, the sparrows, the
    crocuses, the sunlight —
Already over so why act as if I can change anything with worry.
I am determined not to be done in by the future any more than by
    the past.

I believe what I've lost is not the sum total of who I am
Or the only theme for my remaining days on Earth.
Dead parents
Dead lovers
Dead pets
Dead dreams
Dead, dead, dead, everyone and everything dead, or so it seems,
Doesn't matter at all.

Regrets
Wrong choices — really, terrible choices –
Years consumed by fear and loathing
Trying to be someone I wasn't
Such that the decisions of my youth were, I see now, made for
    another
Who was middle-class respectable and eager to don a suit and tie,
Also doesn't matter at all.
I didn't stay in Amsterdam in 1985
Or drop out of law school in 1986
Or move to San Francisco in 1997,
All the paths untrodden.
Now as I walk away from being a lawyer,
Watching myself here from there
Be an old hippie when I never was a young hippie,
I forgive myself for having become something and someone
    I didn't want to be.
It's okay, though — what I did do, what I didn't do –
Everything in this beautiful life of mine is okay.

We are here for a very short time.
Fifteen years in the 5th century
Thirty in the 15th
Nine decades in the 21st.
Whatever we're given is a blip, a footnote in time.
Our attachment to fleeting things and people and places is all we
    know
But not all we are.
We can love creatures of all kinds,
Like birds and cats, turtles and dogs, people and butterflies and bees.
We can love things, too,
Like tulips and rainy days, Van Gogh paintings and long lonely walks.
We can love what we love and still be free
From wanting more than we're given
Or pining for what we'll lose

By accepting that we're already dead,
Standing now in a faraway place looking back on our lives
Deciding whether during every day we were kind
    and brave and true.

Outside the Window

We were once in love
Now we love each other
Offering kindness
Unconditional
A knowing
An accepting
Without need to name it
Without need to own each other.
We'd been alone
Both of us
Pandemic descending all around
Like that 14th century horror show,
Witches burning at the stake
As punishment for the pestilence,
Funeral pyres dotting the landscape
This time called refrigerated morgue trucks,
People desperate
Again
To not become
One of the dead.
We needed
To touch
And drink
Another
During this our second plague together.
Last plague for us
Gay men burning at the stake
As punishment for the pestilence.
Now we are thirsty vampires
Witches not burning
Conjuring hope with our flesh.
Our bodies older now
More wrinkled
Sagging
Still familiar.

We came together this time
On a rainy Sunday,
The face masks made of leather
Stayed on at first.
Our limbs entwined
Hungry
Groping
How hard we were
Two old men
But not so old
Young actually
By the standard of witches.
I entered you
As you begged for it
I loved the begging
The carnal longing
How deep could I go?
It went on for hours.
The marijuana helped
To lose ourselves
In a place far away
From the disintegrating world
Outside your window.
We wanted more
Forbidden mouths
Your mask came off first
I was afraid
But my mask came off, too.
You kissed me
Lips
Tongues
Breath
End of the world sex,
Like after that September day
When the buildings came down

And we came together
Needing the body of someone we knew
Pressed against us.
Always when the end seems near
We come back together
Because with death in the streets of our city
My bed
Your bed
Is a safe place to demand life,
Which is for the living.
And we want to live
You and I
Always
No matter what is
Outside
The
Window.

Sunday in the Park for George

We were still afraid to assemble outside
When the police killed George Floyd
Before our eyes.
It looked like a snuff film
But was business as usual
That day in the heartland
When George Floyd died.
"I can't breathe!"
"Please!"
"Mama!"
George Floyd begged
As he was murdered
Over and over
On our screens
Before our eyes
Before our eyes
Before our eyes.

I was done sitting at home
After three pandemic months
That felt like years
So I grabbed two face masks and out I went into the streets.
I walked Seventh Avenue in search of a crowd
And found a pack of stormtrooper riot cops
Ready for battle.
Secure in my privilege,
Middle-aged and white,
I followed the cops to Washington Square.
With clubs in their hands
They remained outside the park
As I walked past them,
Joining thousands of people
Inside the park
Furious and masked.

While helicopters whirled and roared above in the sky
Suggesting a war zone
I gave myself over to the energy of the crowd
And felt among the swaying bodies
A deep sense of love
And an absence of fear.
You couldn't help but feel it,
Understandable ire expressed as intoxicating love.
I was a 56-year-old white man
Weeping into my face mask,
Entranced by the beauty of the diverse, angry crowd,
Moved by the young Black voices
Speaking their pain through bullhorns with rage.

Beyond the lush, verdant trees
I could see the perimeter of cops
Surrounding the park
Guns at the ready
Clubs in their hands.
In the middle of the crowd a person
Dressed as Spider-Man
Roamed round the fountain,
But these activists with their bullhorns
Were the only superheroes we needed I knew.
Amidst the chants of
"Peaceful Protest!"
"George Floyd!"
"Black Lives Matter!"
A jazz band played protest music.
Grizzled old-school Village guys,
Black and white,
Unmasked while they played,
Made music together
As a young woman nearby

Banged her drum slowly.
Then suddenly all went quiet
Descending to our knees
As one giant organism
Kneeling on the ground
Creating sacred space by our actions in that park,
Electricity running from person to person
Demanding justice
Demanding an end
To the killing of Black people.
The sun at that late-day angle left everyone,
Cops and protesters and bystanders alike,
Squinting, dazed, off-balance
In the celestial light
Of courage and truth.

The F Word

Standing on the subway platform
Waiting for the F train
Delancey Street bound
Hot summer night
Sweating through my mask
Station smells of rotting flesh
Like a corpse left unfound in a stifling apartment.
Faggot
He yells
Faggot
Again,
I turn my head,
Yeah you
Faggot.
I stare at him with a fury
Refuse to divert my gaze
From this screaming maskless man
Refuse to cower
As others walk away
Refuse to fear what might come next.
A giant rat nearby
Stands on its hind legs
To see what all the commotion is about.
It is 1975 1978 1984 1986 1991 1992 2003 2017 again
The verbal bashings of my life
Leaving me each time
Defeated
Traumatized
Angry
Confused
Hungry for revenge.
Not this time
Stepping forward
Refusing to run away
Lowering my face mask

Yelling back
I AM NOT AFRAID OF YOU!
Silence
Another step forward
YEAH YOU
I'M NOT AFRAID!
(Don't have a gun
Please don't have a gun
Don't pull out a gun)
GET THE FUCK OUT OF HERE!
What happens next
In this place
Where I have never been before?
My pulse is racing
My heart is outside my chest
On the filthy platform floor
Next to a puddle of urine.
An eternity in seconds
As I don't walk away —
West Village man killed in gay bashing
The headlines would read —
But up the stairs he goes
Yelling faggot all the way.
I can hear him still
I can hear them all
Each and every one of my bashers
From grade school 'til today.
An old man
Frail and shaking
Comes out
From behind a column,
Looks at me
With tears falling onto his mask
And softly applauds.

"Thank you," he says.
"I thought he meant me so I hid.
Thank you for being brave."
"I'm just glad he didn't have a gun,"
Is all I say to the shaking, clapping man
As the F train comes into the station
And takes me,
Shaking also,
From the West Village
Far away
To the Lower East Side.

Maya Lin's Ghost Forest Rising

I enter sacred space,
Forty-nine tall coastal Atlantic white cedars
Towering amidst the towers,
Hauled from the Pine Barrens of southern New Jersey
To this patch of green between the Flatiron and the Empire State.
It is like walking into the high nave of the Cathedral at Chartres,
Bright afternoon light flooding through the leafless branches
Far above me in the sky.
In a city of ghosts this *Ghost Forest* rises,
A symbol of dead ecosystems and environmental collapse
On an island where people paved over the ecosystem a long time ago.
In Spring '21, my fellow New Yorkers,
Many still masked
All in need of healing and rebirth
React to the ghost trees
By touching, even embracing them,
Sitting on the ground in ones, twos and threes against them,
Several children holding hands and dancing around them.
A veritable faerie forest out of *A Midsummer Night's Dream,*
Within the trees I feel as mischievous as Puck, as open and
    transformed as Bottom.
I place my hand on the bark of one cedar and hold it there,
Surprising myself with this intimate and unexpected gesture.
Similar to a Christmas tree in the corner of my apartment
These trees are not usually there, I know,
And being among them summons real joy.
That they are dead matters little to my being with them.
As I said, New York is a city of ghosts.
I suppose all cities are
But this island-city between two rivers contains my ghosts.
I am used to moving through them
And having them move through me,
So when ghost trees rise in a neighborhood park
Suggesting dead woodlands once thriving
I think about what the artist wants to say with her installation,

Then have an experience
Both solitary and communal
With forty-nine new ghosts
In a city of millions.

East Village Summer Evening (August 2021)

East Village summer evening,
Last of the sun over Avenue B.
Community Garden on Sixth Street
Dripping with vines
Verdant
Flowering
Lush from all the rain
A secret sanctuary garden
Where aging hippies congregate
Face masks dangling.
Sluggish bees
Exhausted from the day
Rest in the humid twilight air.
Spoken word
Drifting
From the stage
Mixes with the tired bees
As the aroma of marijuana
Comes in fresh with the breeze.
The sad season hovers just ahead.
As September approaches, I sense it every year.
I hear a siren
Closer
Closer
Closer
It passes,
The artist resumes.
This tropical night –
"Feels like New Orleans!" I hear someone say –
Makes my skin warm
My pandemic body hungry for contact.
Words
Recited by poets
Wafting
Touching

Caressing
Our souls
Substitute for arms and lips and breath.
The wooden bench below me
Hard
I brace myself,
Hold tight to August.
My city
Cradling me this moment
Reveals
Magic
And
Endless
Grief.

Whatever Comes Next (December 27, 2021)

It has gotten very quiet
Again
Like April of 2020 quiet
But without the birdsong
Because it is winter.
The loudest sound on Jane Street
This afternoon
In the middle of a city
My city
Is a cat
My cat
Snoring on the bed.
No traffic
No car horns
No people walking by below.
The quiet weirdness descended suddenly this time.
We thought we had left it in the past
The quiet
But it followed us here to this new place
We carved out for ourselves
Amidst the ruins of the old place.
The old place and the new place
Look the same, really,
But we don't look the same
When we look out
Or when we look in.
Another sound has joined the snoring of my cat.
The steam heat hissing warmth has arrived from the basement.
It was eerie at first
When the quiet came back
Though not sad
The cat and I
We are not doing sad anymore.
In fact, we made a pact when all this began
Back in 2020

To pretend our sliver of an apartment was a spaceship
Like Doctor Who's TARDIS
Bigger on the inside
Knocked off course
Hurtling through space.
That we're alone again in the ship
The cat and I
During this Christmas surge
Troubles us not in the least.
When the quiet returned
I sighed
The cat sighed
I suppose we all sighed
Alone in our ships
Resigned
Hurtling through space,
And waited once more
For whatever comes next.

Dark

I love when it gets dark early.
As night descends late afternoon
The summertime illusion of happiness is stripped away
And I am left with the cozy aloneness of my hopes and my losses.
The tea kettle whistles while a fire roars
If only inside myself.
This blue and white sweater has moth holes
But it reminds me of younger days so I pull it over my head.
Steam heat hisses from the radiator
While the cat tries to get close without getting singed.

I hear the buzzer.
It's him
This is vampire time
The hour of illicit midwinter rendezvous.
Summer sex is hot but winter sex nourishes the soul,
The body warmth of another keeping me alive
As if we were stranded during a blizzard in a broken-down car
And need to make love to survive.
Afterward, sprawled together naked on the bed,
The Mountain Goats singing from my laptop,
Belgian things strewn about
Draped over chairs and teetering in precarious piles around the room,
I offer him the moth-eaten sweater because he says he is cold.
He pulls it over his head and torso
While I rise to make tea again.
I don't want shirtless men in cutoff shorts frolicking in the sunshine.
I prefer the bundled-up truth of wintertide with its absence of light,
A penis, balls and pubic hair protruding from below a sweater.

I don't deny I'm afraid of the dark
But I am not afraid of being afraid
So nighttime arriving during daytime
Doesn't depress me in the least.
Ultimately, people left alone in the dark

Unraveling the great mysteries of their lives
Are a challenge to the notion that we are not, each of us,
Magnificent winged-creatures capable of flight.

Walking to Alphabet City

When sadness descends it becomes a battle to get out of bed
A battle to shower
A battle to dress
A battle to turn on the radio
A battle to scribble some words and say I've written today
A battle to walk downstairs and check the mail
A battle to pay the bills
A battle to feed the cat
A battle to scoop the litter box
A battle to make the bed
A battle to make breakfast
A battle to make lunch
A battle to make dinner
A battle to not give up,
Though I'm not sure what giving up looks like.
When my life feels inelegant and exhausting
I put on a pair of nice pants and good shoes
And drag myself down four flights of stairs to the sidewalk outside my building,
Then walk and walk and walk.
I try to walk off the sorrow
From the West Village to the East Village
Looking at the faces of the other sad people I pass on my way to Alphabet City
Where they don't have all the letters
Just some of them
A and B and C and D.
Between the letters sits Tompkins Square Park
Waiting for me to seek refuge
Amidst the trees and the benches
The squirrels and the dog walkers
The drug dealers and the old Ukrainian men.
Who am I to be sad when there is so much sadness everywhere?
I ask myself because I believe that I am not entitled to my despair.
Truthfully, it is not a question of entitled.

The compounded losses of my life are enough to justify
Closing the curtains and crying under my mother's wool blanket
That she wrapped herself in when she was sick from the chemo.
I believe it is a question of not wanting my despair,
My mean, gray, overwhelming despair that robs me of joy,
Showing up and reminding me of all I've done wrong
And all wrong that was done to me,
Egging me on as I repeatedly pound myself with both fists
Until I am bloody and raw and broken.
I don't want to be my own worst abuser
So I search for healing
Of my mind and soul and body
By walking
From one end of my village to the other
Where the park awaits
And assures me
The healing has in fact already begun.

Gingerbread Castle

Oh, sunny summer Sundays when I was a boy!
That handful of years we had together as a family of four,
My earliest memories
I can count on one hand.
In my father's black convertible with the red upholstery
We would drive north and west
To Gingerbread Castle in Hamburg, New Jersey.
I remember a photograph of my father
Holding two little children — me and my brother — a giant
 lollipop looming behind.
I remember that day — vaguely — like an old home movie playing
 in my head.
After my mother snapped the picture
I fell and skinned my knee while skipping.
My father carried me as I cried,
Never telling me not to cry
Never telling me five-year-old boys don't cry (or skip),
Because he was not that kind of father.
He was a kind father who bandaged and kissed our bloody skinned
 knees.

Gingerbread Castle is now an archaeological site,
A ruin of Jersey antiquity,
Haunted with the ghosts of dead fathers soothing skinned knees
While gingerbread turrets and ceramic lollipops peel paint like
 frescoes in Pompeii.
The towers of the castle rise behind a chain link fence,
Isolating the grounds, marking them a no-man's-land,
Reminding me of the abandoned amusement park near Chernobyl
With its rusting bumper cars and enormous Ferris wheel dripping
 vegetation,
The ground beneath contaminated for the next 20,000 years.
That is how long it will take, I know,
Until Gingerbread Castle releases its hold on me.
For 20,000 years,

Spanning many more lifetimes than this,
The storybook castle of my childhood
Will unleash fallout from my absent father,
Disappeared by the universe
While I was still a six-year-old boy prone to bloody skinned knees.

A Cat and a Man

Once upon a time
In a city of millions
A cat and a man
Spent days turned weeks
Turned months turned years
Together as one
On a street they called Jane.
The man loved the cat with a reverence reserved
For the deepest loves of one's life
But had no idea that he and the cat had been here before,
And after their lifetimes
Forgot one another
Only to find, each incarnation,
Their way back once more.
In the Irish Dark Ages
On wild untamed bogs
When the man was the man and the cat was the cat,
A fairy cat of Celtic lore,
The man loved the cat
As some kind of god
And young they both died
Fledgling souls on the bog.
During the 14th century
Somewhere in France
A deadly plague raged
Of fever and sores.
The man was the cat and the cat was the man
Alone in a village ravaged and burned.
They had just each other
For all those long days,
Brutal, feral, desperate, bleak days.
Then still in France
Centuries later
A revolution arrived
Disrupting their lives.

The cat was the cat again
The man was the man
The cat watched the man taken away
Leaving the cat to mourn his last days.
In Flanders near Ypres many years later
The cat was the man
Who dwelled with the man living now as the cat
In a cozy thatched house
By fields lush with poppies
As melodious larks flew high above,
Quiet lives lived
On what would become
A war's western front.
When the cat then a man
Drowned in the mud,
One of 7000 killed
In the Fifth Battle of Ypres,
The man as the cat
By himself wandered
Among those Flanders Field poppies,
His teeny heart broken
Like so many others.
Which brings us to now,
21st century New York,
When the cat as the cat
Made an improbable trek
From Kentucky up north
And was saved by the man,
Though it was really the man
Who was saved by the cat.
And so it will continue
The rescuing
Each of the other
Again and again
As cat and man

Then man and cat,
Changing those roles
Back and forth
Forth and back,
Until Earth life ceases
The incarnations end
And stardust they become
Cat and man.

Old Man Inside His Cat Suit

I knew for a week our earthly time together was up
As his body weight dropped and he hid under the bed.
He's like a 90-year-old man, someone said,
I suppose as solace.
But it's sad when 90-year-old men die, too,
Because as the life force drains from their nonagenarian bodies
And they prepare to exit stage left
There is a laundry list of things that will leave with them.
For this old man
Inside his cat suit,
My little boy
My noble familiar,
That list included sleeping pressed against me,
Sitting on the windowsill watching the spring birds dance
From tree branch to tree branch,
Licking me as he groomed himself
Because he was not quite certain where he ended
And I began.
Nor was I
Certain of where I ended
And he began.
He began.
He ended.

Memory-Beetle Circus

My house is infested with memory-beetles,
Insects that have made their way into the woodwork and copper
    pipes
With a single-focused task,
To devour the house from inside out
By making me see things I'd rather put to rest,
Stripping my sweet abode down to its skeleton frame
Like locusts swarming and descending,
Voraciously consuming my verdant fields without shame.
I am not a morning person
I am a person mourning
For things and creatures and places and moments
So, I don't need these memory-beetles leaving their larvae hidden
    here and there,
Metamorphoses waiting to happen in all my nooks and crannies
Including that secret room behind the stairs,
Forcing me to relive life's lesser moments
As well as each and every loss,
Distorted in my brain by the infestation to no longer reflect what
    even really happened
Or remember accurately how much the cost.

I would call the exterminator
But that seems cruel
Even unjust.
I want these dream-state bugs gone from my waking life
Though not if it means they'll nowhere ever again exist
Once reduced to ash and dust.
I must find a way to live with them
As they scurry and fly about.
Pay them no mind
I tell myself,
You only think they can hurt you
You only imagine they will eat all the support beams
And make the house collapse.

I have decided to form a memory-beetle circus
Not unlike with fleas.
Yes, more excruciating
For the ringmaster
Who will of course be me,
Looking weirdly steampunk dapper
In a fancy thrift-store top hat
And red tailcoat to my knees.
The memory-beetles I'll attach to little carts
Get them to perform spectacular acts of agility
And death-defying feats of strength.

Eventually — once the show's perfected —
I will take it on the road,
Amazing crowds with how my memory-beetles
Juggle
Sword swallow
And saw each other into fours.
I am excited by my ingenious plan,
For even if this desideratum does not come to pass
These memory-beetles, I know, will never be the death of me
They won't eat the beams and joists
My house will not collapse.

(Please note no fleas or memory-beetles were harmed in the creation of this poem.)

Singing to My Ghosts

I am haunted by everything.
By breakfast and lunch
My childhood
The dead.
I am haunted by all that I saw
And all that I thought I saw,
The things that were
And the things that didn't come to pass.
I stand with ghosts,
Some holding my hands
Some trying to push me down the stairs.
I have endeavored to make friends with these ghosts
By singing that song that calms me and amuses them,
That song about looking at clouds
From both sides now
From up and down
And still somehow. . .
Ghosts love Joni Mitchell.
The hand-holding ones begin to swing my arms
In a merry playful way,
Then let go so they can stop the others
From hurting me as they try to shatter my vertebrae.
Let him sing
They say without speech,
Telepathically warning
That if the dangerous ones kill me
There'll be no more Joni Mitchell,
I will stop singing.
Alone they'll end up
The hand-holders warn,
Without the boy
Without the songs
Without my breath of life
Allowing them to stay in this world
They long to never leave.

I am safe so long as the hand-holding ghosts remain vigilant.
I am safe so long as I remember all the words,
And never stop singing
Songs by Joni Mitchell.

Our 9/11

Fourteen years after The 9/11 was our 9/11,
September 11, 2015,
The last night you were home with us
Home with me
Home with our cat Jasper.
You went to the hospital on the twelfth day of September
And died on the seventeenth.
During those last days in Mount Sinai
Before I was certain the end was near
You, I think, were certain.
You said that you did not sleep
The night of our 9/11,
You told me that you watched me sleep
While Jasper slept spread across my chest
Thinking it would be the last time in life
You ever saw this sight,
Which always brought you such joy.
I told you that wasn't so,
Promised you'd see us that way again — who knows, maybe you
    have —
Because I could not wrap my mind yet around the idea of you
    being dead.
Now it is 9/11 once more,
September 11, 2022.
Jasper is gone — he died in July –
And I am alone in the apartment
Feeling deep sorrow along with regret
Because death always brings regret.
I watch on TV the same old footage
We watched together in 2015 of The 9/11:
Planes and buildings
A sunny blue sky
People
A dust cloud from the buildings crashing down.
In 2022, 2001 seems forever ago,

The buildings, the planes, the sunny blue sky.
2015 seems long ago, too,
When you left me and Jasper,
Left us staring at the door
You would never walk through again.
I wonder how I will create something new for myself.
I have been wondering that for seven years now.
How
How
How?
Another person
Another cat
A different life I cannot imagine yet,
Happiness allowed,
So that on 9/11/23
I find myself
Living less alone
Less lonely, too,
Because we never know, do we,
What awaits us just ahead?

I Walked by a Coffee Shop

I walked by a coffee shop the other rainy gray day and looked in
   the window.
As one might imagine,
I was surprised to see myself sitting there,
Just sitting there with my coat off and my hat on next to a cup of coffee.
I was holding a pen, staring at a blank piece of paper.
I'd never caught myself out like this before
So I stepped back to avoid being seen.
It was weird how I didn't want me to see me.
I suppose the situation was awkward
And without precedent.
Truthfully, I looked sadder than I thought I would,
Maybe older, too.
Then something made me sit up and smile and I looked younger
   for a moment
As I wrote something down.
I was happy to see me excited by one of my thoughts,
Like, good for you, me.
We're going to be okay.
Everything is going to be okay.
I debated in my head whether to reveal myself to me,
Walk in and sit down and strike up a conversation,
But I was afraid to enter the coffee shop and begin that dialogue.
I wonder what I would have said if I had asked me about love
And loss
And regret
And longing
And aging
And sex
And dread
And joy
And death,
Except I didn't.
I could see myself in the coffee shop writing feverishly
And did not want to disturb

The sudden spurt of creativity
Or honesty
In case I was answering the questions I wanted to ask.

Turn of the Centuries

From time to time
I time travel into myself
Where the centuries reside,
Peeling away my prior selves
Until I get to the first I,
Who had no way of knowing
All that was coming
Over the next 3682 years –
So very very long, sigh.
I am fortunate this incarnation
To understand these things.
If I had this knowledge before
During earlier lives
Those memories have been buried
Somewhere deep
In my subterranean archive.
The way I see it,
Earth is not just an evolving planet
Existing in a physical plane
But a laboratory for spirits
To have a human experience
Again and again and again.

3682 years in the past it was 1659 B.C.
And the last of the woolly mammoths lived
On an island called Wrangel in the Arctic Ocean
Between the Chukchi and East Siberian Seas.
That's how long I have been getting it wrong
Only to possibly learn now how to get it right.
Of course, I could be off with this calculation,
I might be much older
You never know.
Was I ever Neanderthal
Before I was Homo (sapien)?
An apex predator with surprisingly elaborate funeral rites

And a prominent brow.
Those long-ago lifetimes I scratched and clawed to stay alive.
In my more recent lives, I scratched and clawed as well.
I have not stopped being a vulnerable mammal in a dangerous world,
But I have stopped blaming myself for the danger
And what I did to survive.
I have forgiven me
Everything
I ever did to anyone,
Including what I did to me.
They did not give out instruction manuals
In the ancient world
No more than they do today.
Though it's hard to imagine
Our brutality
Then or now
Was really the only way.

Little Edie Feeding Raccoons Wonder Bread

I am watching *Grey Gardens*
Again
On my laptop,
Sitting at my desk
Next to the large window in my apartment,
The one overlooking the honey locust tree that grows on Jane
 Street.
The sun comes
The sun goes
Reflecting my face on the computer screen
Then not
As cloud cover passes.
For a moment I see me there in the attic with Little Edie
Amongst the debris,
Stoic and strong
Staunch one might say
Maybe out of her mind
Wearing the best costume for the day
Feeding raccoons Wonder Bread.

Oh, Edie.
The situation is unmanageable, and you must cope,
But you don't patch the roof
You don't call pest control
You don't find a solution.
You climb the stairs to the attic clutching the plastic Wonder Bread
 bag
With its blue and red and yellow polka dots,
Then feed the raccoons dinner.
You decide to do nothing about your circumstances except live
 with things,
Accept them
Raccoons and all
Exactly as they are. . .
Oh, Edie, I understand.

I also know what you don't know as we stand here in this attic.
You will emerge from the bramble and ivy and ruins
A star at 58
Determined to live life always on your own terms,
Your skirt effortlessly, flawlessly transformed into a cape.

The Invisible Man

I did not know I would become a superhero
With the power to be invisible
Once I lived six decades
But here I am
The Invisible Man
Riding the subway and walking down streets
Teeming with people moving quickly
Incapable of seeing me.
I choose to believe it's me and not them,
That I have willed myself invisible
So I can stealthily move with ease
Around and among the Screenavores,
Strange creatures craving dopamine
Born of the union between fear and longing
Who I believe might stop breathing and die
If someone cut the electronic umbilical cords connecting them
 with their phones.
While these Screenavores focus no farther than the palms of their hands
I move with grace and agility amidst them,
An aging gazelle
Able to avoid detection,
Safe from harm
Standing at intersections muttering to myself
About how the city has changed,
Remembering the eighties and nineties
As if they were dearly departed friends,
Because they are.
When this thing we're calling the 21st century arrived on the scene
I was originally all for it,
Then the planes crashed into the buildings
The wars began
The fascists reappeared
The climate heated up
The chain stores killed all the sweet little shops
And my beloved city-state New York

Became Dystopia-on-Hudson,
Another suburban bedroom community
With glass towers and traffic and rats.
I can report on all this because the invisibility allows me to see things
Unavailable to the visible.
Though I want to be clear
I am not angry
About the dystopia or the invisibility.
I was prepared for the former by the movies of my childhood.
Soylent Green is people!
As for the latter,
I like the freedom of not caring whether anyone is looking at me,
Neither judging nor desiring me.
There is no show to put on in public anymore
For the audience is gone.
But I am far from sad about this,
Let me assure you,
Because not every human gets to outlive their youth.
I knew hundreds — there were millions — disappeared by a plague
Terrifying and grim
That put all the gruesome fairy tales to shame.
Hansel and Gretel never met a witch,
Just America unmoved by Hansel dying of AIDS
As Gretel sewed a quilt panel for him during his last days.
And what about those multitudes of young people
Who also met dear Hansel's fate?
Like me they should have lived to be invisible,
Graceful aging gazelles rushing to catch the train
Dodging the Screenavores
Cursing dystopia
Nodding to another invisible person
In acknowledgment of the situation,
That they must figure out how to be old
Navigating a very different world than the one in which
    they were young.

The Cattery

Here in the cattery at the animal shelter
Early every Thursday morning
I emerge from the bustle of the Lower East Side to begin my shift.
When I enter a room where the cats have free range
Some climb up on the catwalk close to the ceiling
While others haltingly approach me
As I begin to sweep and mop and scoop litter,
Rubbing their tiny noses against my legs.
I call them by their names as I give them fresh linens,
Covering their perches and beds with clean plush towels,
Like the chambermaid in a magical feline Holiday Inn.
As I move among them I softly, gently speak.
I tell them they are safe.
I tell them no one will hurt them again.
I tell them they will never be hungry, never be alone.
I tell them they will each find a home.
I tell them they will know love.
I assure them that everything will be okay.
I know I am talking to myself as I talk to them
In my soft, gentle voice,
Assuring myself
That everything will be okay.
And then one day he is there amidst them,
Bolder, more demanding than the rest
With his tiny nose
Rubbing against my legs.
He will not stop pestering me,
This tough gray and white street cat from the Bronx.
When my shift ends
He presses his face to the glass door as I walk away,
And this goes on for weeks
Because I do not know yet if I am ready to bring a new cat home
Until one day when I find myself asking him
If he wants to come home with me.
This is how I get a new little boy.

This is how life continues.
This is how we both move on
Together
No longer alone.

Wouldn't Hurt a Fly

I lived with a fly once for 45 days,
15 days longer than the average fly stays.
He appeared in the apartment in the middle of May
Buzzing from wall to wall to wall to wall
Staring at me through his two simple eyes
Made up of 6000 compound eyes
And if I'm being honest, for a fly seemed kind of gay.
I named him Fly
When I realized he wanted to stay
After numerous attempts at trying to shoo him away.
I wonder if he named me Man and called the cat Cat,
Which would have been a completely reasonable thing for him to say.
As for he
I don't know why not she
Or they.
I suppose I view each fly as possibly Jeff Goldblum
Who I believe is decidedly him, not her or them.

The cat and I would sit on the bed
While Fly always took the wall
And once we got to know each other
The three of us would chat about when metamorphosis might take hold,
Making one of us (or all of us) into something we weren't possibly
    prepared to be at all.
The cat fantasized about being a bird
Though not the kind that ends up in a large roasting pan,
While Fly waxed poetic about becoming a man.
I confessed I was well into the second act of my play,
But would be willing to learn new lines if my character was
    rewritten and changed.
"We can change ourselves on the inside any time," said Fly.
The cat nodded in agreement and then asked me why
I wanted to change because he (the cat) loved me as is just fine.
"Thank you," I said to the cat as I snuggled my nose 'gainst his head,
"You always make me feel better about life, lessening my dread."

Then one day in late June, on the eve of Queer Pride,
I found dear, sweet Fly dead,
Lying supine and expired in the tub
Like *The Death of Marat* by Jacques-Louis David.
As in the painting, Fly died scribbling a note
Thanking me and the cat in the words that he wrote
For all that we did
Giving him a beautiful life,
Believing that he, a fly, could be anything he desired,
And he returned that support to us when we tired.
Rest in peace Fly
You were a wonderful friend.
Next life if you're human, or even still fly, stop by again
And we three will break bread,
Fly, Cat, and Man.

Under a Gilded Age Gazebo

I strolled into a community garden on the Lower East Side
Tucked away off a street named Elizabeth.
The garden looked from certain angles like steamy Savannah
And from other angles like Paris, France.
The air smelled of pear trees and rose bushes approaching peak bloom
As birds swooped low and called to one another
Amidst my fellow summertime Sunday afternoon strollers.
It felt like a 21st century version of the Seurat painting come to life,
Though no monkey on a leash,
Just one man in a fedora walking a cat.
Hydrangeas and black-eyed Susans climbed the statues and stone
    bird bath
While I anguished over whether my poem was good enough
To share with the assemblage of New Yorkers surrounding me.
I volunteered to read first
Get it over with, I thought,
Like tearing a bandage.
Under a Gilded Age gazebo,
Designed by Olmstead
During another age of robber barons riding roughshod
Similar to our own,
I momentarily froze
Afraid to share the poem on my phone in my hand.
As it circled the gazebo, a kind playful sparrow sensed my fear
Calling to me in a low sparrow voice
That only I could hear.
"Read the poem!" the sparrow said
Before soaring toward the treetops,
Leaving me to summon my courage, find my voice,
And add my poem to the din and tumult of the Lower East Side.

As Daffodils Arise and Forsythia Bloom

There is something thrilling about a rainy early spring day
Walking through the foggy morning glory of Central Park.
Beyond the park the world is on fire, I know.
Smoke rises just past the Dakota
While my feet sink into the splendor of wet green grass.
It's not my imagination,
I can smell distant wildfires and a republic burning
As I stop before Bethesda Fountain and bow my head to the angel,
Then continue across Bow Bridge toward the Ramble.
I've decided to linger in the park and walk the circumference of
    the lake,
Allowing raindrops to run down my eyeglasses
And blur my vision behind streaky mist.
This April rain falling from the gray sky invigorates,
Quenching the May flowers' thirst while they are still in the earth,
Quenching my thirst for rebirth, for reinvention.
Resolutions were made months ago when the new year arrived,
But it is hardly possible to reinvent oneself
While the snow falls
While the wind howls
And January creeps along
Slowly becoming February.
Reinvention follows the crocuses
As daffodils arise from their slumber
And forsythia bloom,
Vibrant yellows sweeping the landscape
Making people giddy with joy despite that smoke in the distance.
When the tulips open it may be too late.
There is always only a small window
For rebirth to take hold.

A Lush Green Spring as Democracy Dies

It rained for 40 days and 40 nights
But I never built an ark
For the squirrels and pigeons, rats and cats,
Deciding that the voice of God inside my head was just not that,
Not God at all but only me trying to make more busy work
To give my life meaning
In the face of increasing repression
From vicious wicked plutocrats.
It was a strange time when it rained and rained and rained
Falling-from-the-sky-sorrow
Like the nuns warned us about in grammar school
Should the saints and angels ever grieve today what's heading our
    way morrow.
"Some bad shit's a-coming!"
Screamed a shoeless man out of his mind
Clearly actually quite sane on the train
Claiming he would flee the city on his own to hike Mount Kilimanjaro.
At that point the water was to our ankles
Everywhere we walked
And I thought for a moment the end might be nigh
But then I balked
At this notion that an ocean would downpour from the clouds
To destroy all our hard work
Under a two-hydrogen one-oxygen atom shroud
Of acid rain and angel tears submerging the city of New York.
The rain stopped as suddenly as it began once 40 days passed
Revealing sunshine where for some time we only saw gray,
Though we'd been unnerved by the deluge
So had no idea how long this respite would last.
As I roamed the streets and alleyways without an umbrella above
    my head
Noticing vegetation vivid green and otherworldly
I questioned if planet Earth was still where I was wed.
How could there be such beauty reflected in the lingering puddles
While Democracy dies,

Taken off life support,
Leaving the lives we were used to living
Really most sincerely dead?
It's that point in the movie where everything's unalterably changed
As I curl up under the covers of my bed scrolling for spoilers,
Ironically, hoping I might once more against the windows
Hear that comforting sound of torrential rain.

Afterlife

They say a spirit survives its human's death.
Once a body has been
Crushed
Smashed
Knocked around
Riddled with disease
Aged beyond repair
Done in by despair
And endless loss,
This thing called a soul
Jumps from the corpse
Embraces its freedom
Becomes again spirit
Rushes toward a light.
Other spirits
Dressed again in mother, husband, lover, child, cat, dog, friend skin
Swarm returning spirit,
Willowy see-through people and pets
Stepping into and out of one another
All becoming
In their unconditional love
One enormous light.
But the life just lived,
Our lives
That's us
That's where we come back into the picture,
That life gets put on trial
So lessons can be learned.
Returning spirit doesn't care.
After all, it is now a spirit again,
Without accountability
For what it once again put a human through,
All part of spirit's eternal journey
Just one lifetime
Among ten thousand

Or maybe more.
Returning spirit should be arrested
Returning spirit should be put on trial
For joyriding
Not just in my body
But in my personality
In my consciousness, too.
Stealing my life like a '63 Chevy with a punched ignition,
Driving donuts in the parking lot behind Burger King
Unconcerned that I am suffering
For spirit to have this reckless experience.
See, these eternal beings
These shimmering reeds of vibrating light
They will not be us,
Like smiling Stepford wives
Wheeling shopping carts
Through cosmic supermarkets
In wide and floppy hats.
Returning spirit will remember
My fear
My hunger
My regret
My shame
My trauma
My grief
My passion
My wandering
My finding
My accepting
My days of easy joy that made me glad I'd been born at all.
But though returning spirit will remember that it had been me,
Returning spirit will no longer be
My fear
My hunger
My regret

My shame
My trauma
My grief
My passion
My wandering
My finding
My accepting
My days of easy joy that made me glad I'd been born at all.
One day I will cease to exist
As me
A person
Who likes to be alive.
And out of my corpse
Will emerge this other being,
Soul then spirit,
Eager to return home
With tales of this latest adventure
For the other spirits to hear and enjoy.
I was once a caterpillar
Spirit will say to itself
As it soars back to that place
Of willowy see-through vibrating reeds,
A place
I
As me,
Exactly as I am
This incarnation,
Will not be allowed
To
Ever
See.

Desire for Wings

I have this feeling I might live
To be a very old man,
And if I have any say in what comes next
I'm frankly not eager to be human again.
I know I won't be me,
Whatever
Whoever
I get to be,
But another version of me.
I want to be
A witness
A watcher
A whisper-in-their-ears comfort
Evoking black-and-white Berlin angels
Invisible to adults
Visible to children
Flying through the city
My city
Not Berlin
New York City,
Sitting at the top of the Chrysler Building
Amongst the art deco gargoyles and steel eagles,
Swooping down like a celestial Superman
When an overwhelmed human just can't go on
Even one more day
Under the weight of 22nd century pain.
I won't long to be human
Like those Berlin angels
Listening to Peter Falk describe the orgasmic pleasure
Pairing a cigarette with coffee.
I've smoked cigarettes
I've drunk coffee
I've been fully human,
With all the horrific agony and ecstatic joy that brings.
I will be content

In my vintage overcoat and slicked back hair
To exist in this city next time without wanting at all,
Just be here
In my solitude
Soaring amidst the buildings
Touching down on rooftops
When a human calls for help,
Visiting now and then the Rose Main Reading Room
At the New York Public Library
Like the angels in the film
Where I can read *Anna Karenina,*
Great Expectations,
Tess of the d'Urbervilles,
One Hundred Years of Solitude,
I Know Why the Caged Bird Sings,
Along with the humans
By gently grazing the side of my head to theirs.
I think that is why reading is one of our great loves,
Because we subconsciously sense the angels pressed against our temples —
The thinnest part of the skull —
Feeling less alone as the words from the page enter our minds and theirs.

So, it is settled.
Next time angel I will be,
Without longing
Without bills
Without suffering or difficulty.
If next time you decide to do the same as me
Be an angel in America
Or somewhere overseas,
Let's meet one day
On the Chrysler Building
And find new ways to aid

All the anguished
Burdened
Oppressed
Humans
Yearning
To
Be
Free.

Acknowledgments

I want to acknowledge so many who made this book possible, which I sometimes refer to as a poetry collection and sometimes as a memoir. You are welcome to think of it as either, since it is a collection of 63 poems that together tell the story of my life. There are 63 poems because that is the age I am turning in 2026, the year this book (my debut poetry collection) is published. In addition, 1963 is the year I was born. The collection begins before 1963, however, at the dawn of all creation since that's really where all our stories begin. The first poem is an erasure poem. *The Book of Genesis* [1:1-1:31] is the source material for this poem in which words have been erased from the text in an excavation to uncover the horror story underneath, a tale of monsters and mayhem that must be recognized along with life's abundant beauty and joy if we are to be true to this human experience we all live.

In 2021, as we emerged from the pandemic, my friend Dan Leibel recommended I read a poetry collection by Sharon Olds titled *Stag's Leap*. I devoured the collection in one sitting, blown away by how it told the story of the end of the author's thirty-year marriage through poem. I had written two novels, but I'd never written any poetry. At least not poetry I'd ever want anyone else to read. Around the same time, I began taking memoir writing workshops via Zoom with Donna Minkowitz, a brilliant writer and teacher as well as a colleague from ACT UP (AIDS Coalition to Unleash Power). I took Donna's workshop five times in a row and many of the essays I wrote in that workshop evolved into poems in this collection. At a certain point, I asked Donna if I could submit poetry for some of the workshop assignments. She said yes, informing me that the only requirement for the workshop was to write memoir, not what form that memoir had to take. For the next four years, I wrote these 63 poems, uncertain they would ever be published by anyone.

Then in 2025, as I racked up rejections from literary magazines and poetry contests, my friend since we graduated from Lafayette College in 1985, Bob Pursell, got an earlier version of this collection into the hands of another Lafayette graduate, Angel

Ackerman, the founder of Parisian Phoenix Publishing located in Easton, PA, the home of Lafayette. Angel read the collection and decided she wanted to publish it, becoming (if I may say) my angel. So, there would be no published collection without Bob and Angel and good ol' Lafayette. I want to thank them for everything, as well as Gayle F. Hendricks and Nancy Scott at Parisian Phoenix, to whom I am so grateful.

   I want to thank everyone who gave me their permission to write about them, whether named or unnamed, including Craig Houser, Jay Pinkerton, Ann Northop, Alexis Danzig, Jamie Bauer, and my cat Sebastian. And I thank all those friends and family no longer with us who show up throughout these pages, including those deceased humans (and animals!) to whom this book is dedicated at the beginning, including Richard Giglio, Howard Pope, my parents, William Raymond (Ray) Black and Winifred McParland Black, and Stephen Bernstein, who sadly died on Halloween morning just as this book was about to go to print. I am so glad that I shared with Stephen before he died the poem *Little Red Cabin on the Hill*. He loved it and said it perfectly captured the spirit of the cabin. I think it perfectly captures the spirit of Stephen, too. He is missed beyond measure.

   Thank you to my brother Kevin Black since many of the early poems from childhood about the loss of our father are his story, too. Thank you to my sister-in-law Jennifer O'Donnell as well as my nephews Ian Black and Lucas Black, who always make me feel less alone and much loved in this life.

   Thank you to Donna Minkowitz, Alvin Eng, Ron Goldberg, and Ben Shepard, incredible writers all, for taking the time to read the collection and write some thoughtful words about the book. I am so touched by what each of them had to say about these poems.

   Thank you to all the writing teachers I have had over the years, including Alvin Eng, Robin Miller, Scott Alexander Hess, and Carolyn MacCullough at Gotham Writers Workshop, Karen Moulding at East Village Fiction Workshop, Cindy Tran at Brooklyn Poets, and of course Donna Minkowitz.

   Thank you to everyone who read one or more of these poems or just listened to me talk about the collection and gave helpful feedback, encouraging me to continue writing, including Elka Krajewska, Jackie Rudin, Jennifer Bartlett, Sandra Abramson, Karen Dinsmore, Mark Jacobson, Dan Leibel, Jay Pinkerton, Coleen Cahill, Stephen Short, Virginia Vitzthum, Cherie Acierno, Susan Freedman, Linda Sokolski, Dixie Beckham, Dennis Helewa, Damon McParland, Tom McParland, Sheila Hickman, Patricia Hubert, as well as every person who ever attended a writing workshop with me.

Thank you to John Bean, who has helped me unravel and understand my life, making peace with all of it, so I could ultimately write about it here.

Thank you to Yvonne Brooks at McNally Jackson Books and Joseph Reiver at Elizabeth Street Garden. The summer poetry series they run at Elizabeth Street Garden on the Lower East Side was the first place I ever publicly shared my poetry. Some of the poems in this collection were written specifically to be read as part of that poetry series. I will always be grateful to Elizabeth Street Garden and will fight for its continued existence as a vital public green space in New York City.

And thank you so much to Tariq Danzig, who conceived, sketched and drew the incredible artwork on the front cover of the book after reading the collection's eponymous poem *The Night of Swaying Grass*. Tariq is a brilliant, talented artist, and I was very lucky to get him to design the cover. You should hire him, too.

I mentioned him above with the other writers offering blurbs for the book, but I must again thank Ben Shepard, who has become my dear and much-loved friend. We have read each other's work and offered honest feedback to one another over the past several years. He made me believe more than anyone else that I could publish a collection of poetry, and that I could publish a memoir, and that I could in fact do both at the same time.

I understand what an extraordinary opportunity and gift it is to have a collection of poetry published at the age of 63 that tells my story: the big moments, the small moments, the loss, the love, the sex, the death, the people, the cats and dogs. This is the story of one life, my life, told in poetry. It is a story of childhood loss. It is a story of grief. It is a story of coming of age and of coming out.

It is a story of resilience and reinvention, a story of discovery and optimism and hope. And it is a story set firmly in New York City, the place I was lucky to reach so I could live my life as an authentic and whole human being. God bless New York City, always and forever.

About the Author

Born and raised in northern New Jersey, R. Diskin Black graduated with a BA in History from Lafayette College in Easton, Pa. He also went to law school, but nobody wants to hear about that. He is the author of two novels, *Zombie Scout: The Diary of Jack Sullivan* and *Ethan Weiss and the City Between Two Rivers*. He lives in the West Village of New York City with his cat, Sebastian.

www.ingramcontent.com/pod-product-compliance
Lightning Source LLC
LaVergne TN
LVHW011946070526
838202LV00054B/4829